Help for Remarried Couples and Families

JFL Judson Family Life Series
Jan and Myron Chartier, editors

Help for Remarried Couples and Families

Richard P. Olson and
Carole Della Pia-Terry

Judson Press ® Valley Forge

HELP FOR REMARRIED COUPLES AND FAMILIES

Copyright © 1984
Judson Press, Valley Forge, PA 19482-0851

Unless otherwise indicated, Bible quotations are from the Good News Bible, the Bible in Today's English Version. Copyright © American Bible Society, 1976. Used by permission.

Other versions of the Bible quoted in this book are:

The Revised Standard Version of the Bible copyrighted 1946, 1952 © 1971, 1973 by the Division of Christian Education of the National Council of the Churches of Christ in the U.S.A., and used by permission.

The New English Bible. Copyright © The Delegates of the Oxford University Press and The Syndics of the Cambridge University Press 1961, 1970.

The New Testament in Modern English, rev. ed. Copyright © J. B. Phillips 1972. Used by permission of The Macmillan Company and Geoffrey Bles, Ltd.

Library of Congress Cataloging in Publication Data

Olson, Richard P.
  Help for remarried couples and families.

  (Judson family life series)
  Includes bibliographical references.
  1. Remarriage—United States. 2. Remarried people—
United States—Psychology. 3. Stepparents—United
States. 4. Remarriage—Religious aspects—Christianity.
1. Della Pia-Terry, Carole. II. Title. III. Series.
HQ536.047 1984   306.8′4   84-813
ISBN 0-8170-0991-4

The name JUDSON PRESS is registered as a trademark in the U.S. patent Office.
Printed in the U.S.A. ⊕

To my husband, Henry
For my children, Kristin, Kelly, and Bob
For my stepson Hank and his wife, Judy
And in memory of my stepson Michael
Together we suffered, grieved, struggled, grew, and
finally became a family
Carole

Editors' Foreword

With the publication of *Help for Remarried Couples and Families*, by Richard P. Olson and Carole Della Pia-Terry, Judson Press launches a series of books on marriage and the family for contemporary Christians. The purposes of the Judson Family Life Series are to inform, educate, and enrich Christian persons and inspire them

    a. to become acquainted with the complex dynamics of marriage and family living;

    b. to pinpoint those attitudes, behavioral skills, and processes which nurture health and wholeness in relationships rather than sickness and fragmentation;

    c. to consider marriage and family today in light of the Judeo-Christian faith.

As editors of the Judson Family Life Series, we are committed to making available the latest in family-life theory and research and to helping Christian families discover pathways to wholeness in relationships. Every attempt will be made by the authors to apply new insights to the realities of daily living in marriage and the family.

Volumes in the series will focus on the stages of marriage, divorce and remarriage, parenting, the black family, and nurturing faith in families. Each will be designed to deal with specific issues in marriage and family living today.

Help for Remarried Couples and Families is the first book in the series. Out of their research and experience, Mr. Olson and Ms. Della Pia-Terry have written a timely book that provides practical guidelines for those who remarry and for the families they bring together.

Richard P. Olson serves as pastor of the First Baptist Church of Boulder, Colorado, and has a pastor's concern for the remarried and their families. As a scholar he has sought to bring to his readers the best insights available.

Joining him as a coauthor is Carole Della Pia-Terry. Pastor Olson married Carole to her second husband, Henry, thereby helping to create one family out of what had been two. Dick and Carole decided to use their experiences, their learnings, and their skills to write this book together, so that others might benefit from their new knowledge.

It is with a real sense of joy and celebration that we introduce you to the Judson Family Life Series and to Olson and Della Pia-Terry's book on remarriage.

Jan and Myron Chartier
Eastern Baptist Theological Seminary
Philadelphia, Pennsylvania

Contents

Varying Family Heritages; Loyalty; New Family Members' Space; Power in the Remarried Family; Communication with Former Spouse; Death of Former Spouse; Importance of Child's Contact with Both Natural Parents; Adjustment of Children to Different Life-Styles; Helping the Child Belong in the Stepfamily; Structural Issues Which Cause Stress; Use of Time to Relieve Stress

By Way of Introduction

We'd like to introduce ourselves to you and tell you what we hope to accomplish in this printed conversation with you.

Dick is a pastor (also a husband and a father) who has worked with many couples anticipating remarriage; he has helped them plan their weddings and has offered them support and counsel as they established their remarried families.

Carole is remarried, a mother, and a stepmother. She was divorced and is now married to Henry, a widower. When Carole returned to college after her divorce, she started out in a business course, then switched to a sociology major. Her advanced sociology courses gave her an in-depth understanding of the subject of remarriage and stepfamilies.

Though we (Dick and Carole) had known each other slightly in the past, we came to know each other well after Carole and Henry asked Dick to be the pastor for their wedding. We shared with each other some of the joys and struggles of establishing a remarried family. (We tell you the story of that in chapter 8.)

Out of this interest in establishing a remarried family, we conducted a series of discussions on remarriage sponsored by a group of churches in the community. Since then Carole has given many talks and seminars on the subject. Out of these experiences came the desire to share what we had discovered with a wider audience. And so we decided to broaden our knowledge by talking to many remarried people and reading widely, and now we share the results of our search. (Incidentally, when we use the term "we" in this book, we are expressing opinions that we share. At some points Dick speaks specifically from his pastoral experience and uses "I.")

In this book we want to discuss many ideas with you. First, we undertake some introductory tasks: unmasking the destructive "myths" about remarriage (chapter 1); exploring the estrangement from church and faith that some remarried people feel (chapter 2); examining the variety in remarried families and helping you to characterize your marriage and family (chapter 3). Next, we discuss readiness for remarriage from the perspectives of the individuals (chapter 4) and the couple (chapter 5). We go on to explore the four most important topics we found in our investigations: remarried-family structure (chapter 6); children (chapter 7); financial management (chapter 8); and dealing with conflict (chapter 9). Finally, we look at some of the long-range aspects of remarriage as the remarried couple and family go through progressive stages of growth and development (chapter 10); then we discuss some long-term issues and our conclusions (chapter 11).

We struggle with vocabulary. Terms used for the new family that emerges when two previous families combine include the following: "stepfamily," "remarried family," "blended family," "reconstituted family." We don't like any of these terms, but lacking a better one, we will use all of them interchangeably.

We write both for the widowed or divorced person and for the single person who marries either a widow(er) or someone who has been divorced. We write for persons considering remarriage (to whom we will probably seem overly pessimistic) and for persons already remarried (to whom we will probably seem overly optimistic). If this is how each of these groups respond to this material, we will have sounded our intended note—the note of realistic hope.

We have written this book for persons in remarriage. We have also prepared a companion volume, for church leaders working with remarried persons, entitled *Ministry with Remarried Persons.*

But on to our conversation. Let's begin by exploring the myths of remarriage.

1

The Myths and Realities of Remarriage

Remarriage occurs frequently in American society today. Stepfamilies make up a sizable minority of all families in the United States, as these statistics reveal: 30 percent of first marriages end in divorce; 80 percent of these divorced persons remarry; and 60 percent of these marriages involve an adult with custody of one or more children. One-half million adults become stepparents each year in the United States. Between one-sixth and one-third of all children in the United States have at least one stepparent.[1]

When you realize the size of the population of remarried persons and stepfamilies, you may question: if remarriage is so common, why is so little known about it? Why is there a trickle of information about remarriages as compared to the wealth of research about original marriages and intact families? Why are there few support groups and classes for stepparents as compared to the many offered to parents?

Lack of information and support are realities for remarried persons. When we set out on this investigation, we discovered that many remarried people feel alone. They tend to assume that they must make their way by themselves. We felt that something should be done to provide information and support for remarried people. This book is a small step in that direction. As a result of our investigations, which consisted of interviews and reading, we developed another hunch. Our hunch is this: since society does not know as much about remarriage as about marriage, it has created a number of myths about remarriage that folks hope are true. And in our opinion many of these myths are false and destructive and get in the way of building strong remarriages and stepfamilies. The myths express unrealistic expectations. When their lives do not fulfill these expectations, couples wonder, "What's the matter with us?" So we begin our exploration of remarriage by unmasking those myths and exploring the realities in remarriage.

Myth One: "Love is better the second time around"; remarriages will be more successful than first marriages. When people have been married before, so the myth goes, they understand what is involved. Remarriages involve people who are older, more mature, and more aware of what they need and want in marriage partners. They also have more financial resources. Further, the myth continues, remarrying persons know themselves better, are capable of greater love and deeper commitments, and know why they are marrying. Hence second marriages will be better than first marriages.

Reality One: "Love is *different* the second time around." All the characteristics of persons entering remarriage that we have described in the myth *may* be true, and yet, the remarried couple must contend with some other factors that will affect their married love. Consider the most frequently used term in these relationships: "step-"—as in stepmother, stepfather, stepfamily. The prefix "step-" comes from the Old-English prefix *steop*, which means "orphaned" or "bereaved." That rather somber prefix reminds us that remarriage is a relationship born out of grief, the loss of a relationship or the loss of a spouse. Death and divorce are both subjects that are difficult to face, more easily ignored in a new relationship, and often avoided by those outside the relationship. The previous losses and grief, however, are an integral part of the person(s) coming into the new relationship.

Since our society is biased toward the original first marriage and core family, many remarrying couples will have to cope with societal disapproval of their second marriages (at least in some segments of our society). Thus, some remarried couples have felt it necessary to disguise the fact that theirs is a remarriage. This is likely to be counterproductive to the remarried couple's efforts to build a healthy relationship.

Further, as Emily and John Visher point out, "Stepfamilies are culturally disadvantaged families."[2] This is not a negative judgment on the stepfamilies; it is a judgment on a culture that has not learned how to integrate them. As Anne Simon has pointed out, "If you want to indicate neglect, say 'stepchild' and everyone will know what you mean."[3] Such is society's negative judgment of the stepfamily.

So the reality is that two people with a maturing love for each other may find themselves entering an unexpectedly difficult, hostile atmosphere when they launch their remarriage.

Myth Two: The previous marriage *ended* with the divorce or death of the spouse. Whatever the nature of that previous relationship, this myth suggests, it is over and done with; it can be ignored, forgotten, and left behind.

Reality Two: Divorce and widowhood are relationships that continue outside the person and within the person.

Divorce is a continuing relationship between two persons, just as marriage is a relationship between two persons. If there are children of the original marriage, quite probably the contact and negotiation between the divorced spouses will need to be continuous. They will need to address the issues of visitation, custody, normal child-rearing expenses, unusual expenses for medical treatment or education, and discipline. There may be times when the children will want both divorced spouses present: school performances, graduations, weddings, baptisms, christenings, confirmations, and illnesses. The partnership and financial responsibility of parents go on, even after the marriage has terminated.

There are also continuing external relationships to deal with after one's spouse dies, such as

—maintaining the relationship with the dead spouse's family.

—providing opportunities for one's children to be in touch with the relatives from the dead spouse's family.

—making decisions about the objects a couple collected in living, not only a house and furniture but also accessories, antiques, photos, and other mementos of a life together.

But a person will experience more than these external relationships because previous relationships have become part of one's inner life. Memories, both good and bad, live on. Feelings from the old relationship surface from time to time. There is grieving that needs to be done about the termination of that relationship. As one man told us, "I sometimes find myself seething with resentment about my former marriage and taking it out on . . . my present wife. That's not very fair, is it?" He was saying that the previous relationship was still a part of him; he wanted to resolve those inner feelings to build a stronger current marriage.

Remarried widows or widowers have told us that they miss their deceased spouses but find this hard to admit to anyone. After all, they do have new spouses, don't they?

We believe that there are effective ways of dealing with both the outer and inner reality of former marriage relationships, and we will speak of those shortly. We simply point out here that first a couple must recognize the existence of these relationships and accept the fact that they will have some influence in the present relationship.

Myth Three: "I'm marrying you, not your family." An able marriage therapist suggests that when a young man said this to his wife-to-be, he was expressing his ardor but he was also exposing his ignorance!

It has been noted that in a first marriage the sequence of a relationship goes something like this:

—the couple builds a one-on-one relationship;

—the couple decides to have children;

—the couple develops a style of raising children.

In a remarriage these three steps are frequently compressed together. The couple attempt to build their married relationship while simultaneously trying to develop a style of parenting/stepparenting. They do both with tentativeness and uncertainty and have little time to devote exclusively to either of these tasks.

When persons remarry, they enter a complex network of in-laws, former in-laws, former spouses, former spouses' spouses, etc. All of these can have some claim or some influence on a person's time, resources, children, and stepchildren. A remarried person experiences less control over his or her life and is involved in much more negotiation.

Reality Three: A more realistic commitment would be "Since I want to marry you, I will attempt to deal with all those who touch your life and I ask you to do the same for me."

Myth Four: "I love you; so I'll love your children, and your children will love me." This sounds logical and natural, but life just doesn't work that way. To be sure, an occasional child with a crying need for another parent reaches out desperately and willingly. And to be sure, an occasional parent is drawn to the stepchildren as strongly as to the new spouse. But these experiences are rare.

The more usual pattern is that the children resist the new stepparent (we will explore the reasons for this later) and that new stepparents do not easily and automatically feel a great deal of love for their stepchildren. What actually happens is that the myth "I'll love your children and they'll love me" clashes headlong with reality.

This myth has a subsidiary myth. It is this: "When we remarry, the family will be put back the way it should be." Somehow, this myth promises a warm nuclear family that is close knit and caring.

Reality Four: "I will be thrust into a relationship with your children and will need to work at developing it. I'll do it for you and for them, but it will not be easy or automatic." While a stepfamily may look like an original core family and while it may develop into a group of people who have many of the same feelings as an intact nuclear family, a stepfamily is different. At least one person is included who was not in the original family, and at least one person from the original family is no longer there. This means that in the stepfamily at least two sets of family customs, styles, and values must be integrated. It means, also, that important outside persons and influences intrude powerfully into the stepfamily from time to time. In addition, some family members may come and go. So the reality is that a new family style is being created; the old family style is not being restored.

Myth Five: "We will know how to act in this new marriage and family. After all, we have been married before, haven't we?"

Reality Five: Although a remarriage and a stepfamily have some continuities with the first marriage and the original family, they also have many discontinuities. In many parts of the country, stepfamilies are still subject to disapproval, isolation, and alienation. The stepfamily's structure is much more varied than the structure of intact families. Stepfamily relationships are new and untested. These relationships are not "givens" as they would be in intact families.[4] The roles of stepmother and stepfather are not as clearly defined as most of us feel those of mother and father are.

As the Vishers point out, a revealing insight occurs when one visits the greeting card counter. There are cards for brother, sister, mother, father. But there are no cards for stepmother or stepfather!

The reality is that if the stepfamily is to succeed, it will need to be more intentional. More discussion and planning will be needed for its success; it will not simply evolve. For a time it will probably be less spontaneous than an intact family. Yet, this process may contribute to a new family strength.

Myth Six: "We love each other so much that this is going to be easy. Love conquers all."

Even persons who have been scarred in previous unhappy love relationships often hold to the romantic myth that love conquers all. "If we just love each other enough, all the details will work themselves out," so the myth goes. And the myth continues, "And because we love each other so much, there will be no great difficulties in building our remarriage and stepfamily life together."

Reality Six: Forty percent of all remarriages end in divorce during the first four years. Many of these failed marriages have involved couples who entered the relationship with real enthusiasm and confidence that they would succeed. Some remarried people speak of high expectations and low rewards. Many of the couples who have built strong, enduring remarriages remember the first years of the marriage as delicate, difficult, and "iffy." So the reality is that even those couples who start with a tremendously satisfying relationship will have to work and work hard at building good remarriages and stepfamilies.

In summary, the person holding onto the ideas reflected in these myths of remarriage may say something like this: "Love is better the second time around. My previous marriage is over and has no influence on me now. I'm marrying you, not your whole family, and certainly not your extended family, your former in-laws and all. As to your children, I'll love them and they will love me. We will quickly become one big happy family as we get things back the way they were meant to be. And because of our great love for each other, all of this is going to be easy."

However, we contend that the realities of remarriage are more like this: love is different the second time around. It may have depth and maturity that the first love did not have, but it will also include some grief. Relationships from a previous marriage affect both one's inner feelings and one's outer dealings. A previous marriage should be resolved as completely as possible and accepted as a historical fact. Often a person will need to have continuing contact with a former spouse. Further, when one enters a remarriage, one also enters into a relationship with a complex network of people, and this requires vast human relationship skills. In all likelihood a person will not automatically fall in love with his or her new spouse's children by a previous marriage, nor will the children be enthusiastic about getting a stepparent. But if all give the new family a chance, respect, friendship, and maybe even love can grow in time. The new family unit will never be the same as the old intact, core family. Instead, it will be a new-style family, in which some of the present members of the family may come and go. The new family will have to learn new roles, customs, values, games, and recreation patterns. The constant need to work out family matters that were firmly established in the previous marriage can be either very annoying or enriching. (Probably it will be both.) For a time it may seem as though family life has lost its spontaneity and closeness. For a time there may be so much disagreement and discomfort that all wonder if the effort is worthwhile. However, as issues are resolved and persons come to accept one another, the new family may grow to be a satisfactory arrangement to all.

Does the picture we have painted seem overly pessimistic? It is not meant to be; we believe that persons can build successful remarriages, because we know many people who have. We believe that such successful remarried persons are pioneers and that they have much to teach one another. We have gathered the discoveries of many such persons in this book, and we trust that their insights will trigger your own awareness of what you have already discovered about building a strong remarriage.

We believe, also, that one path to remarriage strength is for a couple to face the issues in remarriage; to make their problems and disagreements visible; to look at and affirm their strengths; and to discuss and negotiate their differences. We hope to help you with this process in the following chapters.

Questions for Reflection

1. What myths about remarriage did you accept as truth? Why?
2. What carryovers from your first marriage do you foresee (experience)? How will you (do you) deal with them?
3. Do the children included in your new family resist the new stepparent? Do you know why? How can you (do you) handle this as a couple?
4. What problems do you have that you didn't have in your first marriage? Does love conquer all? If not, what will?

2

Religion: The Special Dilemma of the Remarried Christian

The divorced person who is a Christian and is considering remarriage lives with two questions that other divorced people don't have to worry about. The two questions are: (a) How does my decision to remarry affect my relationship to my faith community, my church? (b) How does my decision to remarry affect my relationship to God? (The remarrying widowed person escapes this dilemma.)

One of the problems with which remarried persons contend is that the institutions of society are so supportive of the original family that these institutions seem to be anti-divorce and anti-remarriage. The church is one of these institutions that is sometimes anti-remarriage. Perhaps it is one of the chief ones.

For example, when a couple ask a clergyperson to perform a first marriage, they assume that the clergy will be willing, unless there are extremely unusual circumstances. But when a couple ask a pastor to perform a remarriage and one or both persons are divorced, they assume that the clergy will be resistant, unless there are unusual circumstances.

As a result, many persons conclude that they will have to choose between their remarriage and their church. Many persons opt for remarriage over the church and elect to be married by a civil official rather than by clergy. Even though once actively involved in their faith community, they withdraw from it with a sense of regret and the feeling that they have been betrayed.

We dare to hope that there is a better option than having to choose between remarriage and a vital religious faith supported by a faith community. We dare to believe that a person can have both!

So let us explore this topic from three perspectives: (1) the remarried Christian and the church, (2) the remarried Christian and God, and (3) the remarried Christian's evolving faith life-style.

The Remarried Christian and the Church

As a person considers and enters remarriage, he or she may have two questions to ask the church of which he or she has been a part: (a) Will you provide the pastor and place for my wedding? Will you celebrate this wedding with me? (b) Once I have remarried, is there a place for me in the life of the church?

In two major bodies of the Christian church, the answer to question (a) is often no. One of these is the Roman Catholic Church. The Rev. James J. Young explains the Catholic position in this way. The Catholic Church insists upon the biblical teaching of permanence in marriage in its law and discipline. It does accept divorce as a necessary solution to marriages that have become destructive, but it urges the parties in a divorce not to marry again. The church provides healing, support, and pastoral care for those suffering from the heartbreak of broken marriages. The Catholic Church recognizes that being married in the church does not guarantee the success of the marriage. The marriages of some people who marry in the Church are doomed from the start because one or both parties are either physically or psychologically incapable of entering into a permanent union. Parties of a failed marriage may apply for an annulment, which is a church judgment that the two partners never had a genuine Christian marriage. Persons granted an annulment of their marriage are free to attempt another "first" marriage with full participation and blessing of the Church community.[1]

To obtain an annulment one must apply to the office of the tribunal of one's diocese and provide written testimony of witnesses who have seen evidence that the marriage was, for one reason or another, invalid. The process of applying for an annulment and receiving a ruling takes months, perhaps more than a year.

Annulment does make new marriages possible for Roman Catholics whose marriages have failed. Some persons do not qualify, and others choose not to enter into the extended process of seeking annulment. Coauthor Carole, a former Roman Catholic, chose not to request an annulment. Her marriage of twelve years, which produced three children and was a marriage in which two people had once loved each other, seemed to her to have been a valid marriage even though it failed. Also, she did not want to dredge up old memories and seek testimony from others. So she obtained a divorce without seeking an annulment. To such persons the Catholic priest must say no when a remarriage ceremony is requested.

The other major body of the Christian church that may well say no to the request for a remarriage ceremony is composed of fundamentalist groups who interpret certain Bible passages (to which we will refer later) literally. They believe that these passages state laws which are intended to be obeyed to the letter. The viewpoint of such persons is that the Bible forbids divorce, except, perhaps, for two reasons: (a) if the spouse has committed adultery, or (b) if the spouse is an unbeliever and initiates the divorce. Then divorce, and quite possibly remarriage, may be considered. Out of these convictions, these clergy must say no to any who do not qualify by these rather rigorous standards when they request a remarriage ceremony.

Other Christian churches and pastors are free to be more responsive. For example, I am a Protestant Christian pastor of a principal denomination. While I hope to be faithful to the magnificent concept of marriage that the New Testament teaches, I feel free to respond to persons who come to me to be remarried. When asked if I officiate at the weddings of remarried persons, I respond, "Yes, but never casually." I hope, by the grace of God, to be of aid in helping two persons experience new life in relationship out of the ashes and grief of the old, dead marriage. I want to be helpful and supportive. Many clergy stand with me in this aspiration. Some denominations give more guidelines than others as to waiting periods, and so some pastors have certain requirements with which they must live. But these are intended to be helpful to assure that remarriages are thoughtful, prepared, well-planned marriages.

To readers anticipating remarriage and wondering if they can find a compatible pastor who will officiate at their wedding, I offer this advice. Visit churches until you find a pastor with whom you feel comfortable. Make an appointment to go see that pastor. Be honest about your previous marital status. Ask if the pastor can preside over your marriage and what expectations the church or pastor would have of you before a wedding could take place. And—this is important—do this well in advance of when you want to be married, at least six months ahead, if at all possible. That way, if it doesn't work out, you have time to work on other options; if it does, you have time to build a relationship with the pastor and to participate in that pastor's counseling process. I don't like to preside over any marriages, first or second, on short notice. The person who calls and says, "You don't know me. I've never been to your church, and I'm divorced and have two kids. Could you come to our home and do our wedding next Wednesday evening?" will get a "no" from me.

Once the couple remarries, their next question is this: "Is there a place for us in the life of this church?" A few churches will need to say no because of the convictions we have mentioned. Many more churches, both Catholic and Protestant, will respond with a door left slightly ajar.

Again consider the position of the Roman Catholic Church. In 1977 the American Catholic bishops removed the penalty of automatic excommunication that followed a second marriage by divorced Catholics. On that occasion, Bishop Cletus O'Donnell said, "The positive dimensions of this action are very real. It welcomes back to the community of believers in Christ all who may have been separated by excommunication. . . . It is a promise of help and support in the resolution of the burden of family life. Perhaps above all, it is a gesture of love and reconciliation from the other members of the Church."[2]

The American bishops' decision did not restore to divorced-remarried Catholics the right to receive the sacraments, but some church leaders are saying that in some cases these remarried persons may eventually participate in the whole religious life of the church, including the sacraments. Father Young suggests that such participation is usually worked out between specific persons and their pastor and involves a conscience search based on the particular details of their previous marriage and the Christian character of their new marriage.

John Catoir points out, "A person's destiny before God is not necessarily based on his juridical standing in the Catholic Church."[3] His reasoning is thus: if an individual were unable to get an annulment, and if that person remarried without the blessing of the church but with good conscience, that person should be able to follow his or her own conscience as to whether he or she can receive the sacrament or not. This new marriage might be termed a "good-conscience marriage."[4] And so he suggests,

When a person is inwardly well disposed to receive and is not living in sin, but is prevented from receiving more because of legal formalism than true justice, it is reasonable to assume that Holy Communion may be received provided no scandal be given in such an act.[5]

Further, many local Catholic parishes, dioceses, and a national organization are offering support groups and information to aid the reconciliation of divorced and remarried Catholics with their church. (For more information write: The North American Conference of Separated and Divorced Catholics, 1100 S. Goodman Street, Rochester, NY 14620.) Divorced and remarried Catholics who miss their church may find the church more open to them than they had anticipated.

Some Protestant fundamentalist churches also allow persons to participate in some aspects of church life but without the full privileges of membership. One couple of my acquaintance was attending such a church before their remarriage. When they informed their pastor of their decision to remarry, he told them he would not officiate at the wedding. He said that if they could find someone else who would do so, they could keep coming to the church. They could sing in the choir but not sing solos; they could not be church school teachers or deacons (spiritual leaders). Since they are people who like to do all those things, they decided to reject second-class membership and look for a church that would accept them as they are.

Bontrager notes that churches have three basic positions in responding to the divorced and remarried. One position is hostility and standoffishness. A church with this position would prefer not to have persons around who are an embarrassment to their perfectionist theology. Someone has used the image that such churches tend to "shoot their wounded," or at least abandon them, if the "wound" is caused by divorce or remarriage.

A second position is tolerance. The onus is put on the divorced or remarried persons to find their own way and seek out their own acceptance.

There is, however, a third alternative—deliberate acceptance and assimilation, initiated by the church. In such a church no one is a second-class citizen. The church attempts to express and embody God's love and forgiveness. The church welcomes these persons into the life and leadership of the church.[6] However, even in these churches the people sometimes may not be supportive because they feel awkward and uncertain about their own marriages and unsure what to do with certain passages about divorce. But if the divorced-remarried person can look beyond the present pain and be patient, there is support and caring that will come in that

Christian community. Perhaps out of sensitivity that results from your own experience, you will be able to help someone else who is divorced, widowed, or remarried. Some persons may need to move to a new church and express their needs there if their old church community is traumatized by their breakup and/or remarriage. But there is a place for everyone somewhere in God's church.

The Remarried Christian and God

The tentative, uncertain response of many churches to divorced-remarried people may be all the harder to take because this callousness triggers deeper questions: "Is the church expressing what I fear, that my decision to remarry is cutting me off from my God? Does God disapprove of my finding a person that cures my loneliness, shares with me my joys and sorrows, and helps me enjoy life again? Did I sin so badly in failing in my first marriage that God doesn't want anything to do with me?" The church's lack of wholehearted acceptance may stir some already existent guilt feelings to a fever pitch.

So let's take a look at this issue. Let us look at Jesus' teaching. Does it suggest that remarriage is always a wrong? Does remarriage take a person out of fellowship with the New Testament God? Then let's come back to our own feelings. What did Jesus say on this subject? What do his teachings mean? The key statements from Jesus are these:

> "It was also said, 'Whoever divorces his wife, let him give her a certificate of divorce.' But I say to you that everyone who divorces his wife, except on the ground of unchastity, makes her an adulteress; and whoever marries a divorced woman commits adultery" (Matthew 5:31-32, RSV).

> And Pharisees came up to him and tested him by asking, "Is it lawful to divorce one's wife for any cause?" He answered, "Have you not read that he who made them from the beginning made them male and female, and said, 'For this reason a man shall leave his father and mother and be joined to his wife, and the two shall become one flesh'? So they are no longer two but one flesh. What therefore God has joined together, let not man put asunder." They said to him, "Why then did Moses command one to give a certificate of divorce, and to put her away?" He said to them, "For your hardness of heart Moses allowed you to divorce your wives, but from the beginning it was not so. And I say to you: whoever divorces his wife, except for unchastity, and marries another, commits adultery" (Matthew 19:3-9, RSV).

To understand the dialogue between Jesus and the Pharisees in Matthew 19, we need to know the Old Testament background they are discussing.

In the story of creation, woman was created to be man's companion and helper. When the man saw the woman, he exclaimed, "This at last is bone of my bones and flesh of my flesh." The passage concludes, "Therefore a man leaves his father and his mother and cleaves to his wife and they become one flesh" (Genesis 2:23-24). The term "one flesh" therefore summarizes the divine intention for marriage. It is undoubtedly a sexual image, but it is more than that. It describes a deep, interpersonal, spiritual harmony and oneness, a commitment to work together to battle all the forces—within and without a marriage—that can pull it apart. "One flesh" describes the divine intention for marriage.

The Old Testament also contains legislation for divorce. (Indeed, divorce is discussed enough in Old Testament passages that it must have been a relatively frequent event.) The most detailed passage on divorce procedures is Deuteronomy 24:1-4. This passage prescribes (or more accurately, assumes) certain procedures when a divorce takes place. This passage was the subject of much debate among Jewish scholars before and during Jesus' time because it spoke of a man divorcing his wife because he had found "some indecency" in her. This extremely vague phrase triggered the debate over the legitimate grounds for divorce. Some schools of thought had a long list of justifiable reasons for divorce, and some a very short list.

In Matthew 19 the Pharisees were asking Jesus, "Whose side are you on in interpreting Deuteronomy 24? Should we have a long list or a short list of grounds for divorce?" Jesus responded by saying, in essence, "I'm not going to get wrapped up in that legalistic battle. I suggest that we go back to the original statement about God's intention for marriage; God intended a man and a woman to be one flesh. You are to build enduring, intimate marriages. When you fail that, you have failed God's intention. And the term for failing in marital and sexual commitments is 'adultery.'"

That is what Jesus said. But what is the nature of his teaching at this point? He is teaching here as he always taught. He proclaims God's reign, God's kingdom on earth. He asks us to live in radical obedience to God, as if the kingdom were right here and now. His statement about marriage and divorce is but one of the deep, all-embracing claims he puts on our lives. It is similar to Jesus' kingdom teachings that we should love our enemies, go the second mile, turn the other cheek, and pray for those who despitefully use us. These teachings are kingdom ideals that we take seriously and that we try to fulfill as disciples of Jesus. We aspire to them, but we never completely fulfill them. That, I am convinced, is how we ought to respond to Jesus' teachings here. Jesus' teaching about marriage and divorce is a call to repentance for our too casual attitudes. These words state a beautiful kingdom ideal of committed, lifelong, one-flesh marriages. Jesus' words are more about marriage and what marriage ought to be than about divorce. Jesus' words are not a new law. He never intended that we read them legalistically and thus decide who can be married and who cannot or who can be in the church and who cannot.

How then do those of us who want to be faithful but who sometimes fail respond to Jesus' teaching? Well, we are never casual or flippant about marriage-divorce-remarriage. If we are in a troubled marriage, we do everything in our power to deal with the problems. If possible, we want that marriage to get better and go on. But if the marriage dies, we accept that death and look to God for grace, mercy, and forgiveness. When, in time, we anticipate remarriage, we look to Jesus' statements about the one-flesh marriage as words that speak to our *present* and *future*, not to our past. With God's grace and help we will give this marriage our ultimate effort, so that in the providence of God *this* marriage can be what God intended it to be—"one flesh."

Now, reader, you may agree intellectually with the things just said but still find yourself struggling with a sense of defeat and guilt in yourself. Guilt has many directions, all related to one another. We may feel guilty toward our former spouse, toward our children, toward our parents, toward God, toward the church, or toward ourselves and our own self-imposed ideals. One highly skilled, professional, divorced woman, who had dealt with all her other guilts, still struggled with a sense of personal failure. She told me, "People tell me I'm an excellent communicator, but I have to live with the fact that I couldn't communicate with my own husband."

Bruce Fisher has noted that in each divorce there is a "dumper," one who chooses to leave, and a "dumpee," the one who is left. Each has a type of guilt; the dumper, because he or she left, and perhaps hurt a spouse and/or children; the dumpee because he or she was unable to hold the attention and loyalty of a spouse.

How does one escape the bondage of this gloomy guilt? There are some things that people have done and found helpful, although no easy automatic answer fits everyone. Here are some ideas for dealing with guilt:

—Stand outside yourself and speak to yourself as you would to a friend.

Wouldn't you be very understanding and supportive of a friend in your circumstance? Then be good to yourself.

—Talk with a trusted Christian friend or counselor. Ask that person to express and mediate forgiveness to you.

—Find a group of people who accept you as you are and affirm you.

—Do something at which you are skilled and at which you can succeed.

—Get your theology straight. This is very important.

The question we are exploring is this: "Am I cut off from God by my divorce and remarriage?" Visualize the Jesus of the Gospels. In particular, visualize his acceptance and forgiveness of all sorts of people: traitors, thieves, prostitutes, murderers, convicted felons, and so on. Hear his words of forgiveness, his prayers for their forgiveness. We believe that Jesus uniquely reveals to us the character of God. Jesus once said and still says, "Neither do I condemn you; go, and do not sin again" (John 8:11b, RSV).

Did God cut you off in your divorce and remarriage? No, but you must realize and accept forgiveness in your own life before the fact that God accepts you *as you are* will have any meaning for you.

The Remarried Christian's Evolving Faith Life-Style

Up to this point we have been discussing church and religion as a problem in the remarried Christian's life. Now we need to consider how the church and faith can be tremendous resources in helping persons build a solid, beautiful, substantial remarriage and stepfamily. Here are a few suggestions of ways in which you can claim your church and faith as resources in helping you to build that new life.

First, when you find the right pastor and church, they can aid you and your partner in planning a wedding that expresses your faith and your commitment to each other. Christians believe in rebirth, in new beginnings, in resurrection. A remarriage ceremony can use these Christian symbols to celebrate the divine possibility of new life growing out of the ashes of grief and loss in the past. Children and stepchildren can be involved in the ceremony, but only if they really want to participate and are emotionally ready to do so. (See the authors' book *Ministry with Remarried Persons* for a more thorough discussion of this subject.) Families can be aided by rituals to accept this new reality, your marriage. Remarriage ceremonies should not be carbon copies of first-marriage ceremonies. You can do better than that, and your pastor and church can help you.

Second, use your spiritual heritage as a way of enhancing your marriage and family. As you become better and better acquainted with each other, tell each other the story of your faith pilgrimage—how it began and what its high points and its low points were. Tell your partner when you feel closest to God and when you feel farthest from God. Tell your partner about your doubts, searchings, and unanswered questions. Tell your partner about the convictions and affirmations on which you bet your life. And listen carefully and respectfully when your partner tells you about his or her faith journey. The one-flesh intention for marriage includes spiritual sharing and acceptance of the other person's spiritual pilgrimage.

Third, do not let your present church preferences tear you apart; rather, let them enrich you. Perhaps you have present memberships in two different churches. This is an opportunity for you and your children to learn about another faith community and its way of celebrating life in God. Visit each other's churches. Ask questions, learn, discover.

Perhaps one of you is active in church life and the other is not. Respect for each other and each other's preferences, plus a little give in each direction, can prevent this situation from becoming a holy war over religion.

Perhaps you find yourself needing to look for a new church home together, possibly in a different denomination than either of your previous memberships. Here also is a fresh opportunity. Many of us know little about churches other than the one in which we were raised. What beliefs, what style of worship, what programs of mission, what programs of service to persons in your family do you want in a church you choose? Discuss these issues together; visit churches and carry on your search together. Finding a new community that feels like your spiritual home may be an enriching opportunity for all of you.

Fourth, explore what rituals, in particular what spiritual rituals, you would like to develop in your new family life. Would you like to say prayers of thanks before meals? or bedtime prayers with the children with the stepparent included? Do you want to have family devotions? ways to celebrate birthdays, graduations, baptisms, or confirmations before God? special family observances for Thanksgiving, Advent, Christmas, Lent, Easter, and other holidays? As a family begins to build its life together, it can explore what experiences and rituals might enrich its life.

Fifth, learn from the suffering you have undergone in arriving at the place where you now are. Out of your experience you have something to give to other persons when they go through bereavement, divorce, and remarriage. You can be extra sensitive and supportive. The experiences from which you are now recovering are some of the gifts God has given you that you may minister to other persons' needs.

Sixth, be an advocate in your church life for programs that support and enrich marriage and family life, whether they are first marriages or remarriages. You are aware of how much effort it takes to build a strong marriage and family, and how much persons need the support and encouragement of each other and from knowledgeable leaders. Again, use this discovery to help your church provide those attitudes and programs that will enrich marriages and family life together.

There are many other ways a remarried couple can use the resources of faith and church to build a stronger life together. They do this with the awareness that God created male and female that they might become one flesh. They do this in the name of Jesus who promised that wherever two or more of us are gathered in his name, he is in the midst of us.

Questions for Reflection

1. Do you consider your present church to be anti-remarriage? Why do you feel that way? Are you accepted by your church as a first-class citizen?

2. What can you do as a Christian to help other people who are experiencing divorce and remarriage?

3. Are you comfortable with the fact that you are divorced and remarried? Can you say with assuredness that you are striving for what God intended a one-flesh marriage to be?

4. What can you share from your own experience with individuals and your church to help others in their struggles to build strong remarriages and families?

3

The Varieties of Remarriage and Stepfamilies

Most people know what a first marriage looks like. They know the make-up of an intact family. Not so with remarriages and stepfamilies. Infinite variety in remarriages is possible. There is so much variety, in fact, that it is difficult to say anything about remarriage that will apply to all persons in remarriage. So let's take a look at some of the variations in remarriages. We will do so by asking you a number of questions that help you characterize your (future or present) remarriage and stepfamily. Then we will discuss them. Here are the questions.

1. What was the previous martial status of each partner?
   Husband was ___ unmarried
               ___ widowed
               ___ divorced
   Wife was ___ unmarried
            ___ widowed
            ___ divorced
2. What are the ages of the persons entering the remarriage?
3. Are the ages of the persons in this remarriage "similar" (less than ten

years apart) or "dissimilar" (more than ten years apart)?
4. Are there children?
___ Neither partner has children.
___ Husband has children by previous marriage(s).
___ Wife has children by previous marriage(s).
___ Both husband and wife have children by previous marriage(s).
5. If there are children, which age groups do they represent?
___ preschool
___ elementary school age
___ teenagers
___ young adults
___ adults
6. If there are children, where are they? Indicate which statements are true.
___ Children are permanently absent because of distance, court order, and/or contentious ex-spouse.
___ Children are largely absent because they are independent.
___ One spouse's children are present nearly all the time; one spouse's children are present for occasional visits.
___ Either or both spouses have joint custody of children and thus have the children approximately half the time.
___ Children of the current marriage are present all the time.
7. How would this remarried family unit describe itself financially?
___ It is so poor that life is a struggle for existence.
___ It has enough money to supply necessities, but there is a constant competition for money for such extras as special lessons, musical instruments, summer camp, vacations, etc.
___ It is wealthy enough for most of the needs and wants of all members of the stepfamily to be met easily.
8. What are the sources of family income?
___ husband's employment
___ wife's employment
___ both spouses' employment
___ either or both have income besides employment (investments, alimony, child support, etc.)
9. How must the family income be used?
___ simply for maintenance of the present family
___ for money obligations outside the present family (alimony, child support, old debts, etc.)

10. How is money managed in this family?
    ___ All money goes into one fund, except for small personal funds for each spouse.
    ___ Each spouse keeps own money and contributes to common expenses.
11. What expectations do the partners bring to this marriage? Is there any way in which these expectations are connected to the families in which each of them were born? Did they have the same expectations for their previous marriages? Were these expectations satisfied or frustrated in their previous marriages?
12. What role does religion play in their marriage and in their family?
13. What are the positive forces outside this marriage? What are the negative forces outside this marriage?
14. What are the positive forces within this marriage? What are the negative forces?

Those are the questions. Let's discuss them.

Questions About Previous Marital Status

What was the previous marital history of each of the partners? How does this previous history affect them?

Each person entering a marriage could have been either previously unmarried, widowed, or divorced. And each of these types of marital history has its influence.

A partner who has *never married* may enter the marriage feeling like a "rookie" who is marrying a "veteran." The previously single person may have more surprises while learning to build a day-to-day life with another person. This will be especially true if the marriage partner has children that the previously unmarried person is expected to aid in parenting. Instant family with no previous experience may be the issue that the previously unmarried partner will have to face.

If either or both partners have been *widowed*, they come with different histories and needs. The marriage may have had problems and pain, but the remaining spouse tends to remember only the good, and perhaps may even idealize the deceased person. This may be particularly true if the widowed person remarries before having resolved the grief of the former marriage. Some frustrated partners of widows or widowers threaten to build an altar and light candles to Saint _____, the "sainted" former spouse who is now dead. The widowed person is apt to have a house full of pictures and other mementoes of his or her former married'life. He or she may have a need to hold onto these mementos and to maintain contact with the dead spouse's family.

The marriage partner who has been *divorced* may need to be in fairly constant contact with the former spouse, particularly if there are children of the first marriage. This frequent contact, which may be punctuated by conflict, serves to remind the couple of the reasons why the divorce took place. There is not much temptation for a partner to idealize the former spouse; in fact, anger at the former spouse may erupt from time to time. Also, the former spouse's decisions and actions may intrude upon the present marriage. As a result, divorced persons may have more feelings of guilt, rejection, and failure to deal with and may be wondering whether or not they could have done something different to make the first marriage succeed.

Each of these previous marital conditions will have an impact on the individuals entering the new marriage relationship and, thus, on the relationship itself. There are eight possible patterns for remarriage from the point of view of the couple's previous marital history:

a. divorced man — single woman
b. divorced man — widowed woman
c. divorced man — divorced woman
d. single man — divorced woman
e. single man — widowed woman
f. widowed man — single woman
g. widowed man — widowed woman
h. widowed man — divorced woman.

This list assumes one previous marriage for at least one partner. If either or both partners have been married more than once, the number of possible variations would be even larger.

A couple might want to discuss such questions as: How do I feel about my previous marital history? about yours? How do our histories influence our present relationship?

Questions About Age of the Marital Partners

What are the ages of the persons who are remarrying?

For the most part, of course, persons entering remarriages tend to be older than persons entering first marriages. The mean age for people marrying for the first time is in the early to mid-twenties. For people marrying for the second time, the mean age is in the mid-thirties. However, there is tremendous variation in age represented by people who remarry.

In general, increased age is seen as a factor that increases one's chances of success in marriage. It is hoped that increased age brings more emotional maturity and greater relational skills. There is an old folk saying to the effect that "youth is a disease from which we are all cured."

Persons entering a second marriage might find it fruitful to reflect upon, and then discuss, such questions as: How much older am I than when I entered my first marriage? What was most important in life to me then? What is most important to me in life now? In what ways am I a different person than I was then? In what ways am I the same? Have I grown? matured?

Are the ages of the two persons in this remarriage "similar" (less than ten years apart) or "dissimilar" (more than ten years apart)? Studies show that there tends to be much variety in the differences in ages between persons who remarry. If there is a large difference in their ages, they may view that difference as merely incidental because they think of each other as peers. However, wide age difference may be a factor in the roles they play. A much older man may be cast in the role of father. Either or both partners may feel that he is wiser, knows more, and should make the major decisions. A couple needs to be aware of the danger of this stereotyping and decide whether or not they want to challenge these roles.

Another result of an older man marrying a much younger woman is that the husband may have children who are close in age to the age of his new wife. This may have implications for his children's acceptance of his wife.

Also, the older husband may be much older than his wife's children; in fact he may be old enough to be their grandfather. This may influence his relationship to his stepchildren. He may be overly rigid and strict or overly permissive and more like a doting grandfather. However, he may take this opportunity as a second chance to be the sensitive father he longs to be.

Since women's life expectancy is still approximately seven years longer than the life expectancy for men, the wife in a marriage in which the husband is much older may anticipate a long period of widowhood.

This discussion is based on the fact that in most age-different marriages the man is older than the woman. It is not meant to discourage persons of differing ages from marrying. It just raises some of the issues such a couple should consider.

Questions About Children

If there are children, what are their ages? Where do they live?

The varying answers to these questions about children underscore the variety that can exist in remarriages.

The most obvious discovery that comes from looking at all the possibilities is that remarried families will not be the same as intact families. Children will probably have more adults in their lives than in intact families. Adults will need to work out relationships with children that are not their biological offspring. In general, the younger the children, the easier this will be. However, people remarry across the age range, and so their children may range from newborn to age fifty or more.

A couple may want to analyze their answers to these questions: What will be the range of the number of people in our household? What will be the fewest number of persons present at one time? the largest number of persons present at one time? How will we, and those who come and go, adapt to this changing scene?

We will speak of all these matters in more detail later. For now we simply ask the reader to look objectively at the remarried family of which she or he is a part.

Questions About Economics

How would this family unit describe itself financially? What are the sources of family income? Where must the family income go? How is the money managed in this family?

Since money is a tangible symbol of power and since power is an issue in many marriages, money resources and money management figure prominently in a remarriage. We will explore this subject in depth later, also. For now, simply identify the economic realities and style of economic management that characterize your remarried relationship.

Questions About "Legacy"

What expectations do each of you bring to this marriage? Is there any way in which these expectations are connected to the families into which each of you was born?

Marriage counselors speak of the "legacy" from the family into which a person is born. This "legacy" is not a financial inheritance. Instead, it is everything else one might get from one's family of origin. Each person carries some physical characteristics from it: vigorous good health or nearsightedness or susceptibility to diabetes, for example. Persons also receive from their families an unconscious understanding of how a family system works, and this "legacy" might be quite different for each of the partners. Individuals may bring from that original family a feeling of being ignored or deprived or unjustly punished. Some persons may have a crying, unrecognized hope that the new marriage partner will do for them all that their parents did not do. When that is true, the marriage is in trouble from the start. A person may be crying out for more than any other human being can possibly provide in a marriage relationship.

The basic question is this: "Am I bringing healthy, realistic, flexible hopes and needs to this marriage, or am I bringing unrealistic, impossible needs to it?" The problem is that *you* may be the last to know the answer. However, if you have had a string of unsatisfactory relationships, you might want to pause and discuss your history and expectations with a good marriage counselor before proceeding to the altar.

Questions About Religion

Many questions about religion can help the couple to identify what sort of relationship and what sort of family life they will have. The major question is "Will religion be a uniting or a dividing force in your family?" Other questions about religion have been raised in chapter 2.

Questions About the Force Field Around This Remarriage

What positive and negative forces *outside* the couple are operating in this remarriage? Examples of such forces are:

—the attitudes of the children of each spouse (the answer may vary from child to child!);

—the attitudes of the parents and family of each spouse;

—the attitudes of each spouse's former spouse and former in-laws;

—the attitude of the community in general and of such particular communities as church, neighborhood, work group, and previous friendship groups.

What other forces could you add to this list that either support your remarriage or cause stress within it? Which forces in the above list could you cross out as nonexistent or unimportant in your marriage? Are the other forces on this list positive or negative? How strong are the positive forces? the negative forces? How will these forces influence your relationship as a couple?

What are the positive and negative forces *within* the couple's relationship that operate in this remarriage? These forces may include:

—the couple's sense of companionship and friendship with each other;

—the couple's romantic-sexual attraction to each other;

—the couple's agreement or disagreement about husband-wife roles and parent-stepparent roles;

—the couple's sense of partnership in raising and disciplining children;

—the couple's shared recreational interests;

—the freedom given each other to pursue some recreational interests that are unique to that person.

Which of these forces are absent from your marriage? Which are positive? Which are negative? How strongly so?

We will be exploring all of these issues again in the pages that follow.

Question for Reflection

Make sure you have answered all of the questions (1 through 14) at the beginning of this chapter.

4

Personal Readiness for Remarriage

Observers of remarriage have discovered that some people enter remarriage before they are ready. This puts a double burden on the couple. They must deal with their individual readiness and their new marriage relationship at the same time. Obviously it would be much more wise to be ready, and *then* to remarry.

What is readiness? How does one recognize it? How does one achieve readiness? In this chapter we begin to search for answers to these questions.

Building a One-on-One Relationship with Me

When we visited with recently divorced or widowed persons about how they were feeling about life, relationships, and marriage, two strangely contradictory themes seemed to come up again and again. "Never again—I never want to risk marrying or trusting another man (or woman) again" and "I can't make it by myself; I must remarry and *soon*!"

When you think of it, both themes are quite understandable. In the latter case the person has experienced marriage as a way of life, an accustomed habit. One woman told us, "I was amazed that after he left I missed Sunday football, and I thought I hated football. I missed making and serving him big dinners, and I thought I resented doing those dinners. I missed being married." Troublesome scars may remain so that the person suffers in loneliness, unable or unwilling to reach out to others. Needful of others, but afraid to trust others; accustomed to one life-style (family) but damaged by that life-style; not ready to make important decisions but forced by the pressures of living into making decisions—such are the emotional dilemmas of many recently widowed or divorced persons. We can see, therefore, that a person needs to build *self-trust* before he or she is ready to make wise decisions about remarriage.

Mel Krantzler speaks of persons who marry to fill "the poisonous needs" that they felt in the first two years after their divorces.[1] What are the poisonous needs?

—I can't manage these kids by myself.

—I can't support myself.

—I need someone to take care of me.

—I just want some good home cooking again.

—I'll show her (him) that I can get along without her (him) and that others want me.

—I'm afraid to be alone.

If such pressing needs dominate, a person can easily confuse *desperation* for *love*. A marriage entered into from desperation starts out with a severe handicap. The person has not married another person; he or she has married an escape. The person has gone into the marriage with impossible needs and demands, which no one individual can satisfy adequately. When the person discovers that the new spouse cannot satisfy these impossible demands, there is an inevitable letdown. Furthermore, if one marries for these reasons, one is marrying into a trap; the marriage is not a freely made covenant with another person. If the person marries out of desperation, that person will feel the compulsion to stay in an unsatisfactory marriage— simply because one's pressing need is so urgently felt—and won't feel the inner strength to negotiate to make the marriage a better one.

All will agree that marrying out of desperation is not a good way to build a new relationship. Each remarrying person should ask himself or herself some hard questions. Why am I remarrying? Do I feel inner strength and joy within me? Am I freely choosing a person in whom I also sense inner strength and joy? Or am I forcing this relationship? If so, out of what needs, what pressures, or what tensions? Am I marrying out of desperation? If your answer to this last question is yes, we urge you to delay. A marriage to the same person at a later time, when you are more ready, will have a better chance of succeeding. Or perhaps this relationship is not right for either of you.

The already remarried person may want to ask: Did I marry out of desperation? If so, to fulfill what needs? What tensions did I create by my expectations and demands? What important issues did I suppress in order to get those needs met? Can my spouse and I talk to each other and renegotiate our marriage by freely expressing our desires, needs, strengths? Can we begin again together? What roles, rules, and rituals have we created? Would we like to change these? How?

Although these questions of relating to another person are important, we first need to build a strong relationship with ourselves. Building a self-accepting relationship has several aspects.

First, one has to accept one's own recent history. "I was in a relationship, and divorce or death has terminated it. This was an unexpected and almost certainly unwanted event. I may want to deny or ignore it, but I admit that it happened to me." This admission is part of the mourning process; and when one makes the admission, he or she is dealing with real grief whether the relationship was terminated by death or divorce. The losses of an ideal or a dream, of a relationship, of marital status, and of "couple" friends are most real! This grief must be admitted, accepted, experienced, and mourned.

A person may be tempted to deny the termination of the relationship and in denying it he or she may be investing a lot of time, hope, energy, money in an emotional "corpse," the dead marriage relationship. Eventually one must cease to invest in this dead relationship and begin to invest in oneself and in filling one's own needs.

The person needs to ask, "What can I do to take care of my needs? How do I nurture my self-esteem, which has been quite badly bruised by what I have just gone through?" In the initial stages, one may be dealing with survival needs. "How do I survive economically; what can I do to increase my income and reduce expenses so that these two balance? Where can I find a job and what can I do? How do I find child care and/or provide sufficient parenting-love-discipline for my children? How can I recruit the children to help me carry the extra load? Who are a few reliable people upon whom I can depend if I need help?"

Those questions should not crowd out these equally important questions: "How can I nurture me, stroke me, take good care of me? What do I really love to do? Are there interests of mine that I have been suppressing because they did not 'fit' my former marriage? If so, how can I get involved in these interests that 'turn on' the real me?'' Perhaps a person loved to dance, but the former spouse didn't dance (or bowl or paint), so that interest was buried. It can be revived now. Perhaps one wanted to go to school or seek employment in a field that seemed fascinating, but "couple" interests prevented that pursuit. The time has come for the person to explore the interests that are uniquely his or her own, interests that hold the possibility of some enjoyment and success.

It may be hard to "get up a head of steam" over such questions immediately following a divorce, however, because one is feeling so negative about oneself. A person feels like a failure because so much personal investment has gone into a marriage that has failed. Rebuilding one's self-concept is a difficult task; it takes much time, specific attention, and energy. Bruce Fisher suggests these steps for rebuilding one's self-esteem.

1. ". . . Make a decision to change." Get in touch with the emotional energy and life forces in you that build rather than destroy.

2. "Change the way you look at yourself." Make a list of twenty things you like about yourself.

3. "Say positive things about yourself aloud to others." Break that deeply ingrained habit that one shouldn't brag.

4. "Reexamine your relationships with others, and make changes which will help you break destructive patterns and develop the 'new you.'"

5. In some way, "Get rid of the negative self-thoughts in your head."

6. "Write positive notes to yourself and pin them up around the house in prominent places." Perhaps these could be taken from that list of twenty things you like about yourself.

7. "Open yourself up to hearing positive comments from others."

8. "Make a specific change in your behavior." Make the change you would most like to make; it could be as simple as saying hello to more people.

9. "Give and get more hugs."

10. "Work hard at meaningful communication with another person." Learn to talk, listen, hear, give and receive feedback, so that the richness of the relationship and the self-learnings can increase.

11. Your needs may be such that to deal with your self-image "you may choose to enter into a therapy relationship."[2]

To Fisher's list, we add a very important item. Find yourself a group of caring supportive people who can help you reexamine your self-image. Up to this point, Fisher has been speaking of a person dealing with his or her own self-esteem. But self-esteem is more than a self construct. One's self-image is greatly affected by interactions or lack of interactions with other people. Becoming part of a supportive group and reaching out to others are important means by which people can examine and nurture self-esteem.[3]

When one has at least begun to work on the issues of self-need, self-care, and self-esteem, perhaps one can come to see *singleness* not only as something thrust upon one but also as a life-style one can choose. A person needs to discover that a period of singleness can be a time to grow as an independent person. A person needs to discover that singleness is not only OK but also valuable and necessary.[4] As one man put it, "When I could enjoy a sunset by myself and know that life was worth living either by myself or with someone else, then I knew I was ready to think about remarriage."

There is a faith dimension to this rebuilding process as well. One who has experienced a divorce may wonder if she or he is rejected and judged by God and may ask, "Is there a future in the faith for me?"

Evelyn and James Whitehead speak eloquently to this point. They point out that Christians believe that God is present in every significant psychological passage, including divorce, "inviting us forward with special graces and opportunities." They continue,

> In the dynamic of our psychological growth (even through failure and sin), God's grace purifies and matures us. In the religious passage of divorce we are stripped of our confidence and our public success at marriage. We die to an important part of our life. Drawn into the darkness of this passage, we are invited to examine its core; to confess our responsibility (whatever it may be) without debilitating guilt; to acknowledge our partner's responsibility without vindictive blame. In short, a divorcing Christian is called to a passage of reconciliation: this includes sorrow, repentance, and forgiveness. It includes, in the Christian dynamic of growth, dying and beginning to live again. Such a passage of pain and grace will leave a person wounded but not crippled. The scars of divorce will make a Christian more sober about intimacy and marriage but will not mark the person as unmarriable. These scars, signs of injury and healing, are not so different from the other scars that mark the body of Christian believers.[5]

In short, in this process of dealing with self, a person needs what James Emerson terms "realized forgiveness," the knowledge that God not only forgives people in general but also forgives every individual and invites each one to a bright and open future.[6]

As a prologue to the rest of one's life, one needs to come to this assurance: "I've come through a hurting experience, and I am stronger for it. I am a special, unique person who is forgiven, growing, and faced with beautiful possibilities. Any person I let close to me will have to be pretty special, too!"

Claiming Freedom in My Options

The previously married person has three possible options in regard to future marriage:

1. I must remarry (because I am not strong enough or complete enough in myself).
2. I must not remarry (because *they* [persons of the opposite sex] can't be trusted).
3. I am free to choose singleness or remarriage (each choice will have rewards and each will have problems).

We believe that persons have two restricting options (1 and 2) and one freeing option (3). We have already discussed the first restricting option; now let us examine the second. The question is this: Is it possible to learn to trust again, and if so, how?

As Bruce Fisher points out, the person who says, "I'll never marry again," is speaking more of oneself, than of the opposite sex. Fisher uses the term "love wound" to describe what such a person is experiencing. "A love wound is the internal pain felt after the end of a love relationship. It is the feeling that 'love equals getting hurt.'"[7] If one is in just such a situation, how does he or she move beyond it?

Krantzler suggests that as people learn from living in the aftermath of a divorce, they may experience four stages in learning to love and trust again.

The first stage is the "Remembered-Pain Stage." The message one sends out in this stage is "Don't come close to me; I've been hurt too much."[8] Each person has an inner timetable. Usually, the thrust for personal growth and relationships will surface within a year, and the person will be ready to move on to other stages.

The second stage is the "Questioning-Experimental Stage." One discovers that one is not alone and that life offers opportunities for acquaintances, friendships, and possibly romances. However, the basic thrust of the person in this stage is to get in touch with other people without making a commitment to one person and to discover that even in carefully distanced, casual friendships, there are warmth, insights, and beauty to be shared.

The third stage is the "Selective-Distancing Stage." On the one hand is the discovery that new relationships can be adventures and the hunger for a deeper, more intimate, more trusting relationship. On the other hand are the fear to commit and the remembered hurt. The signal one sends at this stage is "Come-close-but-go-away-because-I-don't-want-to-be-hurt-again."[9]

A person may enjoy intense personal closeness with another, but then may feel a fear or panic because the closeness is threatening.

Krantzler calls the fourth stage the "Creative-Commitment Stage." At this point meeting people offers promise, not threat, to one's way of life. The signal given by the person entering this stage is "Come closer at your own pace, for I would like to know you better. I will be comfortable with whatever consequences might or might not develop."[10]

Of course, life is never as neatly arranged as it sounds when we describe this process on paper. The description of the process tries to say to a person, "You don't have to remain the way you are. There is possible growth; give yourself time. You may fluctuate between stages; don't worry, many people do."

One may ask, "Just how do I grow in these matters that are so important to me?" There are several things one can do to contribute to one's own growth. (a) Read; in particular, read the books by Mel Krantzler and Bruce Fisher that we have cited in this section. There is much more wisdom in these books written by two gifted counselors with wide experience than we could give in this brief section. (b) Find a support group, either an informal group of a friend or two who have successfully made these adjustments or a larger, more structured group that offers aid and mutual sharing.[11] (This footnote will direct you to ways to locate such groups.) (c) Seek counseling, if necessary. Some may sense the need for a skilled, objective person in addition to friends. Others may sense that they have a rage they cannot let go or a despair about life itself. (d) Give yourself time. Both the writers we have mentioned suggest that on the average it takes about three years to recover from a loss before one is ready to enter into something new with depth and promise. Of course there is no exact time. For a variety of reasons, some people may take more time and some may take less. But in the first years after a death or divorce, a person will do well to ask oneself carefully (and perhaps with the aid of that skilled counselor), "Is this love or desperation?" (e) Claim your faith resources. Sometimes the turmoils and tragedies of life stir us to the recognition that we are not alone. The God we have believed in rather casually, the church with whom we have associated for some time, and the people who have become our friends can all be with us. We accept help when we are in need, and then we are empowered one day to offer help to others.

Questions for Reflection

1. Do you accept your own history? Have you married and then moved on? What are your needs? How do you take care of your needs and build your self-esteem?
2. As a divorced Christian have you died and begun to live again?
3. Have you learned to trust again? What problems did you encounter as you learned to trust?

5

Building a One-on-One Relationship in Remarriage

In the previous chapter we discussed building a personal readiness for remarriage. We turn now to the fascinating subject of relationship building.

Developing a One-on-One Relationship with Another Person

A person does not usually make a general decision to trust other people again. Rather, someone else will call forth a person's willingness to trust. In order to make some things clear, however, let us explore building a one-on-one relationship as though the decision to trust the other person fully has already been made.

How does one get started in formulating a new one-on-one relationship? One starts in the strange, new-old world of "dating." Morton Hunt notes how strange one feels when one gingerly enters the world of dating after being out of circulation for a number of years. However, once one actually starts dating, he or she discovers a great deal of flexibility and freedom in the new dating patterns, which differ in puzzling, perplexing ways from the old. In Hunt's words,

Once the FM [Formerly Married] starts dating, he [or she] rapidly finds that there is great flexibility among the Formerly Married, and that he [or she] can arrange the details of his [or her] dating in whatever way best suits his [or her] own personality, age, means, and tastes. The prevailing philosophy of the subculture, as he [or she] soon realizes, is thoroughly permissive. No one need consent to any suggestion he or she dislikes, but it is not impermissible for the other to have made it. If a man wants to invite a woman out just for cocktails it is not improper for him to do so. If he wants to have dinner with her and then go dancing, she, as the early-rising mother of school children, is perfectly within her rights to suggest a shorter evening instead. An invitation to his apartment is allowable, and is possibly—but not necessarily—an advance notice of an attempt at seduction; an acceptance on her part is no guarantee that she will comply—although she well might. But in their case, there is nothing dreadful about his attempt or her refusal. The rule of life . . . Do what you like . . . expresses the dominant attitude within the World of Formerly Married; short of misusing or damaging another person, almost nothing is disallowed. The emotional needs of FMs are so imperious and their haste so great that they have granted themselves and each other the right to discard most of the impediments of middle-class propriety.[1]

Such a dating pattern thrusts many decisions upon a person who may have been protected for years, decisions about closeness and distance, decisions about sex. (We will speak of these in more detail shortly.) But the dating experience may also contribute to a person's healing, helping one to be aware of one's own appeal, aliveness, attractiveness, and social skills.

In time, short-term, casual dating will not provide what the person senses he or she needs—a deeper, more committed, long-term love relationship. As a person becomes more open to this, he or she may encounter others who have similar readiness, and such a long-term love relationship may develop. Such relationships, even though each one is unique, do have a certain life cycle, which goes something like this:

The Encounter—During this often unplanned and accidental meeting, two persons subtly communicate their status, emotional condition, and interests to each other.

The Wooing—This is the stage for "the pell-mell outpouring of likes and dislikes, experiences and emotions, and most of all, allusions to and outright confidences about their marriages and divorces." The theme for this sharing is: "I have known sorrow—will you comfort me?. . . . I am seeking someone again—is it you?"[2]

The Winning—Recognizing and expressing a deep emotional attachment, the couple becomes involved in romantic and possibly sexual interaction.

Falling in Love—To their amazement, adults find themselves enjoying(!?) the turbulent emotions of romance they knew as youth and the numerous expressions of romantic love they show to each other.

Commitment and Fidelity—They make the decision that they will commit themselves emotionally, socially, and sexually to the other person and will be faithful to that commitment for as long as they stay in this relationship.

Obstacles, Large and Small—Since marriage is the implied goal of this relationship, partners begin to look at each other, each other's faults, and their "fit" or compatibility with each other more carefully. Matters that were unimportant early in the relationship take on more seriousness as the couple consider a permanent pattern. Such issues as partying or staying at home, promptness or inattention to time, neatness or messiness, strict or permissive discipline, careful or carefree money management and many others, come under careful scrutiny and can create obstacles for the couple.

Some couples may choose to go on and marry, either conquering the obstacles or marrying in spite of them. This will be the minority, however, since most love relationships do not end in marriage. For some the obstacles are so great that the relationship must end.

The Break-Up—Formerly married persons, already too well acquainted with the anguish of prolonged breakups, may want to break swiftly and cleanly, although the relationship may have been so valuable to either that this is difficult to do.

Aftermath—Some people are apt to have a recurrence of the same symptoms that occurred when their marriages broke up—depression, insomnia, loneliness. In a slightly less painful and involved way, this break-up is like a death or divorce all over again. Because of the pain of separation, some may choose to avoid commitments that might be hurtful.[3] However, for most persons the positive values of such involvement far outweigh the negative. A person can find it restorative and reassuring to discover the ability to care and feel within oneself. Further, one discovers that he or she was seen by someone as a worthy love object. As a result, he or she may be more ready for remarriage.

Two Issues for the Formerly Married

As one moves into the world of dating and longer-term love relationships, one faces two issues about which we will comment only briefly.

First, one encounters different attitudes about sex today than one experienced when dating ten to forty years ago. Dating partners may imply or overtly propose sex even on early, casual dates. Morton Hunt notes four classifications in regard to sex that seem to exist among formerly married people.

1. Abstainers—those who for personal or religious reasons choose not to have sex.

2. Users—persons who want or need sex from other persons but do not intend any commitment or emotional involvement. In Hunt's terms, these are persons who attempt "counterfeit intimacy."

3. Addicts—persons who are much like users but who attempt sexual conquests with even less relationship and more urgency.

4. Golden Mean—those who choose, or blunder, into some pattern between the extremes represented by the other patterns.[4]

If one is to venture into dating and love relationships in this kind of world, what is one to do? Probably one should begin by looking within oneself and asking "What are the values I hold in regard to sex? Why do I hold them?" The two biblical themes—that (a) sex is the creation and, thus, the very special gift of a loving God and that (b) the expression of sex is to be rigorously controlled—have been communicated to those of us raised within the Christian faith, probably with more emphasis on (b). We were taught that the appropriate expression of sex was within the marriage commitment. Whether or not we actually followed that teaching, we intended to do so.

Perhaps we need now to ask why the Bible and the church emphasize sex within marriage only. The answer seems to be twofold: (a) sex is a symbol and expression of the "one flesh" bond between man and woman; (b) historically, men wanted to be absolutely sure that their descendants and heirs were truly theirs. When one reads the Bible more carefully, one discovers acceptance of other sexual practices: multiple marriages, which were available to some men, and a rather casual attitude, acceptance of the presence of prostitutes, for instance.

Out of such reflection, one asks, "What do I sense is appropriate moral behavior? How do I live out my life in fellowship with my God?"

In answering that question one needs to live with both one's head and one's heart.

We know persons who have chosen the path of abstinence until marriage. However, we have known others—equally devout Christians and faithful church persons—who sensed their own integrity and were able to express themselves appropriately in sexual involvement with a trusted partner to whom they were not yet married.

We were saying that one's values and morality are important parts of a person, but we contend that the Bible does not provide complete sexual guidance for persons in the "formerly married" circumstance. Therefore, as Paul once said in another morally ambiguous situation, "Let everyone be fully convinced in his [or her] own mind" (Romans 14:5b, RSV).

A second issue for the formerly married may be "Shall we test out this relationship by living together?" Persons are doing this in increasing numbers, but is it moral? Is living together helpful to guide me toward an appropriate decision on whether or not to marry this person? Does it help build a stronger marriage bond?

The answer one gives to the morality of living together will probably follow the answer one has given to the previous question about one's own sexual morality. Of course, it is possible to have short- or long-term living together with separate sleeping arrangements, and we've known a few couples who have done this in order to investigate interaction with the children. However, for most persons, living together also means sleeping together.

Not all will agree with Mel Krantzler, but he contends that living together can be a moral, mutual investigation of a long-term commitment in marriage. In order for it to be that, he cautions, a couple should *not* just drift into a living-together arrangement. Rather, the decision should be based on a couple's open and intentional decision to investigate whether they want a close, committed relationship, and if so, whether this is the person with whom to form it. Mel Krantzler did decide to enter into such an intentional arrangement with Pat, the woman who eventually became his wife. They subsequently discovered that living together was an intermediate step in their learning to love again.[5]

Basically, persons can learn two things in such an arrangement. One will be "Can I retain my identity and the important things that I learned about myself while I was single, within this couple relationship?" The other will be "Can I learn to cultivate mindfulness in my relationship with this person?" This means becoming more sensitive to the needs, feelings, limitations, and boundaries of both partners. It also means learning to express feelings, including negative feelings, in a loving rather than hurtful way.[6] The person can discover whether he or she can break old destructive ways of relating and build new ones that sustain a relationship.

As one way of exploring the love relationship, living together is a short-range arrangement by its very nature. It will lead either to break-up or marriage.

Is a living-together arrangement useful in helping a couple to make an appropriate decision about marriage? At this point there does not seem to be any clear, conclusive answer to that question. Some, like Krantzler, would answer yes. Others say that the tentativeness of living together and the commitment of being married are different and that little learning from one applies to the other. Furthermore, since the partners see living together as temporary, they may deny matters that trouble them or postpone issues that they would consider important if they were married. Furthermore, the image of "lover" or "live-in partner" may seem to them to be light and playful, while the images of "husband" and "wife" are loaded with heavy freight from past experiences. Our caution is this: one may not learn as much as one thinks from living together. There may be more discontinuities between living together and marriage than one suspects. A couple who have been living together and are entering marriage may want to discuss the following questions with each other: What do I avoid discussing that is important in our relationship? What do I tend to deny? What do I expect to change after we get married?

Persons with children have further cautions in entering living-together arrangements. The impact of grief and loss on children if the relationship doesn't work out is one caution. The communication to children about their own sexual values is another concern. The goal for each couple is for their decision to be morally based and consistent with the values by which they live.

Building an Honest, Transparent Relationship

There is still another area to investigate in exploring the one-on-one relationship. It often seems that persons in remarriage never learn how to relate. Pessimists contend that many people seem to marry the same kind of person (one with similar problems, viewpoints, life-style, outlooks) over and over again. Sadly, there seems to be some truth here. A pressing question is "How can I marry someone who fits my personality, and how can I relate to that person more effectively than I have related in the past?"

We need to look for a way in which two people can foster integrity and honesty in their relationship from the start. George R. Bach and Ronald M. Deutsch speak of just such a way when they speak of "the pairing system."[7] They see "pairing" as a new way of helping love to begin. In order to understand what they advocate, however, we need to compare it with the traditional courtship system. In courtship, they say, the courter shows his or her best self, accentuating strengths, hiding weaknesses, and seeking to impress the other person. The courter creates a facade in the hope that it will attract the other person. Having assumed a role, the person is more or less saddled with that role. Courters hide their reality because of the fear of rejection. Thus they create the illusion "We are *right* for each other, so we automatically please and fulfill one another. Real conflict must be kept hidden at any price because it would signify that we are not predestined lovers, after all."[8] The fear then is that "Who I really am is unworthy; so I will hide me, my needs, my conflict of interests and needs that I might have with you."

By contrast, they point out, the pairing system deals with fears by facing and resolving them, rather than by concealing them. The message couples share with each other in the pairing system is this: "I am more myself because I know that you see me as myself. I know that the authentic me is the person you love. So I can be that person fully and proudly and with delight."[9]

In the courting system one does "imaging," that is, attempts to create a favorable, striking image. In the pairing system, one attempts to present one's whole self and to be interested in the other person's whole self. In the courtship system, the couple does a good deal of "matching," creating a long list of interests and tastes that match. In contrast, persons operating with pairing-system beliefs do not hesitate to disagree, express different opinions, or state reservations. In the pairing style of relating, polarities (opposites) can be the means for sparking interest and creating enrichment in a relationship.

Those who follow the pairing system avoid the method of "love now, fight later." Instead, partners state their reservations and resistances from the outset. They seek ways to deal with conflict as it arises and to deal with just the subject of the conflict (more on this in a later chapter). Persons using the pairing system see that there is a style of aggression and conflict resolution that is a path to intimacy; pairing partners should seek and practice it from the beginning.

Sensitive pairers are aware of how easily illusion can creep into a relationship, and so they keep checking on whether this is happening in their relationship. Pairers from time to time should share with each other a "state-of-the-union message." This means sharing honestly with each other in response to the question "Where are we now?" in regard to their feelings of attraction, joy, and readiness for commitment; their reservations about each other; their ability to handle conflict, and so on.

In short, the pairing system requires using those principles of communication, conflict, openness, and integrity that aid real and honest relationships. Although partners using the pairing system may struggle to operate in this manner (it is, after all, contrary to the way most people relate to each other), they can say with a fair amount of integrity, "The person I love is the real person, not my image of her or him. And I, not an image of me, is the one who is loved in turn."

Building the One-on-One Relationship in the Early Period of Remarriage

One might hope that after rebuilding one's own self-concept with inner healing *and* reestablishing one's ability to trust again *and* building an open, honest love relationship with another person, *then* marriage itself would be a breeze. Sorry, but that's not true. Indeed, most of the persons we interviewed and the literature we read on the subject reveal that many find the early months and years of remarriage surprisingly heavy and difficult.

There are many reasons for difficulty during this period. For one thing, as Laura Singer has pointed out, once the couple are married, almost everything about a couple's relationship changes. Therefore, a profound and crucial adjustment is to be expected. The couple change from single persons to married persons. For some, the change may be for the better in many ways; commitment, intimacy, permanence, and guilt-free sexual freedom may come with the marriage ceremony. Others find themselves overwhelmed with feelings of responsiblity in what had been a light, playful relationship.[10]

Further, it is quite probable that a tremendous amount of denial has been going on throughout the engagement period.[11] As the couple move from denial to honesty at some point early in marriage, greater differences and adjustment tasks than they had imagined loom before the couple.

People, of course, are not intentionally dishonest during the premarriage time. It is just hard to present one's whole self and see the other's whole self at the same time. This process is apt to be seen more clearly in that total social-sexual-parental-financial-spiritual union that is marriage.

Quite frequently, a person marries only one facet of his or her spouse and expects the rest to conform to that part. [12] One man we know was attracted to his second wife by her lively sense of play, joy, partying. It brought out something in him that he treasured. However, in the marriage relationship he sometimes saw her playful side as evading the responsibilites of living. When she said, "Let's not unpack and clean the basement tonight; let's go to the symphony instead," he found that playfulness irritating, not entertaining.

Even if a person feels that he or she has responded totally to a prospective spouse, he or she should be prepared to see new aspects of that person after their marriage. The marriage counselor frequently hears such statements as "I never saw his rage"; "I never saw her difficulty in handling alcohol"; "I never noticed how tense the children make him"; "I never saw what a spendthrift she is"; "I never sensed his stinginess"; and so on. One needs to be prepared for the unexperienced aspects of the person one is marrying. The decision one must make is this: "Based on what I have experienced of this person, I will risk marriage with her (him). I don't know all, I cannot know all, and that is OK."

Our point is that there are some surprisingly difficult basic adjustments to remarriage. Mel Krantzler uses the phrase "remarriage-shock." He says that just as people experience separation shock when they are widowed or divorced, so they feel a shock when they remarry. Mel Krantzler and his wife, Pat, experienced such shock when they remarried. Fear and emotional turmoil—feelings of nausea, dizziness, and fatigue—overwhelmed them on their wedding day. On their honeymoon they felt they were "suddenly strangers—awkward, clumsy, and tense." [13] It took most of the first week for them to become to each other what they had been before that wedding ceremony. The fear of commitment, the awareness of how much it would hurt if they failed again, the loss-change of personal roles—all this and more entered into Mel and Pat's severe case of remarriage shock.

Once one has dealt with the shock of remarriage, one faces other issues in the early period of remarriage. Singer suggests that there are at least three issues that surface early in marriage. One issue is learning how to handle the discovery that the partners are very different from each other and must find a way to work out the conflicts of wants or needs created by their differences. The second issue concerns learning how to deal with one of the most common differences that couples experience, dissimilar needs for intimacy and closeness. The third issue is learning how to distinguish between togetherness and closeness. Some couples have a feeling that if they love each other, they should have the same interests and therefore do everything together. If they believe this, the desire of either member to do something apart from the other causes much anxiety. But this yearning for sameness is really a distorted concept of marriage. The striving for oneness (complete and constant togetherness) between husband and wife stifles individuality. In such a marriage, couples will likely feel "choked, trapped, and overwhelmed by too much closeness and togetherness."[14]

Yet another issue for the couple is for them to discover what love is and what it is not.

One of the basic problems with marriage today is that our society bases the marriage relationship almost completely on love and then imposes demands on this love that it can never fulfill; some of these demands are

"If you love me, you won't do anything without me."

"If you love me, you'll do what I say."

"If you love me, you'll give me what I want."

"If you love me, you'll know what I want before I ask."[15] (In other words, you will have a crystal ball and anticipate my needs without my speaking of them.)

These kinds of expectations make love into a sort of blackmail. But persons entering marriages (even second marriages) often have such expectations (because, if the marriage didn't work last time, it was her [or his] fault!). The task, then, is to move from unrealistic love to realistic love instead of from fantasy to cynicism and a sense of betrayal.

Unique Issues Early in Remarriage

Much of what we have said to this point applies to the early period of marriage whether first or second. But remarrying persons also have unique issues to deal with.

Emily and John Visher point out that the fact of their remarriage may create some pressures on the couple. Some of the people or institutions in their life which normally would be supportive and encouraging to a first marriage may be resistant to a second marriage, creating yet more obstacles for the couple to overcome. The Vishers note *external* pressures on the couple:

—neighborhood criticism. If one partner moves into the house of the new spouse, neighbors may have a difficult time accepting the newcomer.

—negative response from one's in-laws.

—insensitivity within institutions (for example, schools and churches). Personnel may be unaware that adults with surnames different from those of their children may be responsible for the children and care deeply about their welfare.

—legal considerations, including the lack of legal rights of the stepparent.

There are also *internal* pressures on the couple:

—differences in life-style, which affect both the couple and the children of either person

—bonds that still remain from previous relationships, including those with one's own children, one's former in-laws, "couple" friends from former marriages, etc.

—relationships with ex-spouses

—financial problems

—discipline problems

—tensions between stepchildren[16]

We will speak about these pressures in more detail in later chapters and will also explore the dynamics of the remarriage relationship as it develops.

Clifford Sager and associates have looked at the many strands that the remarrying couple must bring together to establish a successful remarriage. They suggest that the couple analyze their marriage contract. This term does not refer to a formal written agreement but, rather, to the conscious and unconscious expectations that each of the partners brings to the relationship.

Remarrying couples may want to ask, "Starting with what I promised and asked in our marriage vows and including things we didn't mention, what am I asking and what am I promising in this relationship?" As the couple probe this question deeply, they will discover that their "contract" probably exists on three levels of awareness: (1) those aspects they have talked about; (2) those aspects of which either or both persons are conscious but which they have not yet discussed; (3) those hopes, needs, and expectations that are very much part of both partners but of which they may not even be aware.

Remarried couples may find it helpful to explore what they have subconsciously included in their "marriage contract." They may want to do this by themselves, or they may want to seek the help of a competent marriage counselor. At least three areas need to be covered, and some of these may be easier to examine than others. The three are:

1. What do each of us expect in this marriage? A loyal, devoted mate committed to a life-long, romantic, intimate, and exclusive relationship? mutual discipline of children? companionship? guilt-free, enjoyable sex? bearing a child together? etc.?

2. Do either or both of us have inner needs or family issues that will enhance or complicate our marriage? If so, what are they, and how can we deal with them? Are our ties to our own children overly close? Have we achieved emotional divorce from our former spouses? Do we fit with each other on such relational issues as independence-dependence, activity-passivity, closeness-distance, and dominance-submission-equality? Does either carry a heavy load of guilt that influences present behavior? Have our roles (always vague in the stepfamily) been discussed and reasonably defined? Is either one of us troubled by fear of abandonment? How confident or how anxious are we about this relationship? How can our confidence be increased?

3. How do we deal with specific external issues in this marriage? What is our style of communication? Openness, conflict, or negotiation? Do we have cultural or life-style similarities or differences? How do we relate to our families of origin? to ex-spouses and ex-inlaws? Do we have "family myths" about either this marriage or previous ones? How do we celebrate family milestones and holidays? What are our values relating to money, culture, ethics, relationships, religious beliefs and practices, use of time?[17]

Sager and associates have offered a much more detailed analysis of the issues in a remarried couple's contract than we have given. Our summary of the issues, however, can help a couple begin to discover the strengths and weaknesses of their relationship and to identify the issues they need to deal with in order to build their strength as a couple.

Our listing of these issues is not meant to be pessimistic or defeatist. We are simply saying that a person who feels a large responsiblity looming ahead in marriage is in good company and is seeing the situation accurately. To achieve a good marriage takes all the skill development, patience, persistence, commitment, and faith one can muster. But the richness of a good relationship is well worth all the effort. A good marriage *is* possible.

So, read on. We will continue to try to clarify the issues in remarriage and to give you handles to manage these issues in your own remarried relationship. We now turn to structure building in remarriage and stepfamilies.

Questions for Reflection

1. How did your courtship before your second marriage differ from your first courtship? In retrospect, what would you change in the remarriage courtship?
2. Have you decided what you believe about your own sexuality?
3. How do you feel about people living together before remarriage? What guidelines do you see as necessary for living together?
4. In what ways are your ex-spouse and present spouse similar and dissimilar?
5. Did you follow the "courtship system" or the "pairing system"? How?
6. What facet of your spouse did you marry? What surprised you about him (or her) after you were married?
7. What are your needs pertaining to closeness and intimacy? Are they different than your spouse's? How have you dealt with the differences?

6

Building a Family Structure

No one entering a second marriage marries just his or her partner. Invariably, there are other relationships and responsibilities that go along with the new marriage mate. The only variations are in how many persons are actually connected and how complex the new network will be. Complexities arise from the presence and needs of children, from the extended families of both partners, and from the remarriage itself.

We will look at this subject in two ways. In this chapter we will explore family structure. In the next chapter we will discuss children and parenting more directly. In truth, of course, these two areas are never separated, and yet it will be more clear to explore them separately. What are the problems two persons face as they attempt to rebuild a family structure?

Problem One: Remarriage and Stepfamilies are "Unfinished Institutions"

We are using the term "institution" as sociologists use it, to mean those enduring, predictable behaviors that society prescribes. "Institutions" help people know what to expect and how to behave in certain circumstances. While individuals can exercise a good deal of freedom within institutions, they are freed from having to figure out what to do in every circumstance.

Close observers of marriage note that in first marriages and intact families the roles of husband, wife, father, mother, and child are quite clearly defined. First marriages and original families are "finished institutions."

On the other hand, roles are by no means clear in families of remarried couples. Some persons express this confusion by comparisons. Becoming a stepparent is like

—"stumbling along an unfamiliar path in partial or total darkness. . . . Although there are over 35 million other American adults who are stepparents, the path sometimes looks and feels absolutely deserted."[1]

—trying to learn to swim in the deep end of the pool rather than in the shallow end.

—parachuting into an unknown country where you don't know the language, the customs, or the rules, and yet are expected to perform effectively.

—taking a part in a play already in progress. You are given a role but no script; you do not know the plot, and the play has a cast of thousands!

And so, persons find vagueness and ambiguity when they try to function in this new style of family life. Andrew Cherlin notes at least three ways in which stepparents experience this.

First, they sense vagueness in the lack of adequate terminology for remarried family members. What do the members of a stepfamily call one another? What terms or names do they use to introduce family members to others? (More on this in the next chapter.)

Second, they feel unclear about their roles because the legal system provides inadequate support for stepfamilies. Indeed, current law interferes with the establishing of a strong family bond in the new stepfamily in several ways. It does not provide the stepparent with the authority to make important decisions about a stepchild's welfare—even emergency medical treatment. It does not provide the stepparent with any legal rights to custody of the child if the natural parent dies, even if they have had a long-term supportive relationship. Incest laws or taboos do not exist as clearly or strongly in stepfamilies as in original families. Internal revenue rules are vague and difficult for separated or remarried families.

Third, stepparents have this feeling because customs and conventions of family life are deficient when applied to stepfamilies. For example, there is no accepted style of discipline for stepparents to use with stepchildren. Stepparents have considerable uncertainties about appropriate role behavior. Generally accepted guidelines for sharing parenthood among a group of adults have not emerged.[2]

It is not too much to say that the present situation approaches chaos, with each individual remarried family having to work out its own destiny without any realistic guidelines from the society in which it lives. Unfortunately this leads to a good deal of hostility, competition, and jealousy—both between stepparents and children and between stepsiblings—all arising out of the feelings of insecurity, vagueness, and role confusion that exist in our culture.[3]

Prospective or existing stepparents need to discuss the following questions with their new families: "What am I supposed to do ?" "What do I want to do?" "What role does my spouse expect me to take with the children?" "What is my spouse willing to allow me to do?" "How can we work together as husband/wife, parent/stepparent?"[4]

With much discussion remarrying persons may avoid some of the pain and find ways to deal with the rest. Some subtle, hidden barriers to a smooth family life exist because in our society stepfamilies are an *"incomplete institution."* Therefore much attention, discussion, and negotiation will have to be done, much more so than in a first marriage.

Problem Two: Varying Family Heritages Compete in Establishing a New Family Life-Style

Consider the experience of Phoebe and Rick. Phoebe had been married for seven years and had borne two children in the marriage. Then she divorced. She was a single parent for three years. Then she married a widower, Rick, who had one son and who had functioned as a single parent with his son.

When this new stepfamily began to build its life, many different family experiences influenced its decisions:

1. The family Phoebe grew up in
2. Phoebe's first-marriage family
3. The single-parent household containing Phoebe and her two children
4. The family Rick grew up in
5. Rick's first-marriage family
6. The single-parent household containing Rick and his son[5]

Of all the previous family experiences, the experience of the single-parent families may be particularly strong. This might be true because these experiences are the most recent and because sometimes the single-parent family creates a very tight bond, with its own customs and rituals, which are held onto fiercely. Furthermore, children may have been elevated almost to a spouse role because of the needs of the single parent. When their parent marries a new spouse, children may fight to keep that single-parent family unit a closed system into which intruders are not welcome.

At any rate, at least six family experiences were involved as Phoebe and Rick attempted to build a new family style with their children.

Previous family patterns either bump along together uneasily or clash head-on as the new family searches for its own procedures. Differences may emerge over "varying expectations of when to go to bed, where to put the television, how to light a fire, bake cookies, make pancakes, drive a car, and celebrate holidays."[6]

Decisions like these and intrusive family traditions will come up almost hourly as a new stepfamily begins its life together. For example, the family will have to decide such questions as these:

● When are meals served? How large are they? Do we eat meat? sugar? Do we snack between meals? Must children eat all the food set before them? What do different family members like to eat and how is it to be cooked?

● Are pets allowed? Inside or out? Who cares for them?

● Who does what work assignments in our household? How neat must children's rooms be? Whose responsibility is it to keep rooms clean?

● Is TV on never, rarely, often, or all of the time? How loud? What about radios or record players?

● Does the family go to church? What church? Do the members attend church activities? Does the family say grace at meals? What other religious rituals, if any, occur in the home?

● At what temperature is the house to be kept? Can lights be left on? How relaxed or careful are we going to be about energy bills? How clean does the house have to be? Who is responsible for cleaning it? (and so on).

This "family heritage" issue deals with the practical and tangible aspects of daily family life and takes much time and energy.

As part of the family heritage there is an even more basic issue—the issue of loyalty. To what individuals does each member of the family feel loyal? To what family or families? Children will usually feel loyal to their natural parents, no matter what. (Note, for example, the drive that many adopted persons feel to locate their biological parents, whom they have never seen or known.) Children will feel loyal to their family of origin, which may cause them to resist any substitute family. This loyalty may also cause them to strive, for some time at least, to reestablish that family of origin with both natural parents. Loyalty to new adults (stepparents) may develop in time, but it will virtually never take the place of loyalty to biological parents.[7]

Problem Three: Two Family Systems Come Together to Form a New System

Family therapists now speak of the family as a "system." By this they mean that a family is more than the sum of its parts. A family has a network of personal interactions, transactions, roles, rules, rituals, mutual influences, and more. This family system has a powerful influence on the persons within it.

Family process is the total of all the interactions that take place in a family. One aspect of these interactions is the part that rules will play. The family is a rule-making group. Families communicate to their young how the family hopes the young will live within the family and in society. In families, also, certain members play certain roles. These roles are not only husband, wife, father, mother, child, but also clown, martyr, peacemaker, and others. (Family members need to examine to see if they are locked into roles and always play the same roles, whether fitting or not.) In families there are also rituals as part of family process. These are the predictable ways that family members respond to one another in the same setting. Rituals may include religious practices, seating arrangements at the dining table or in the car, or procedures for going to bed, and so on. A family's rituals may be simple or complex.

In the family system there are also at least three "spooky" influences: secrets, ghosts, and mystification. Secrets are beliefs, practices, or information about the family and/or family members that the family does not reveal outside itself. Some remarried families treat the remarriage and the existence of former spouses as a secret. Ghosts are expectations passed on from generation to generation. Husband-wife roles may be such ghosts, and so may unhealthy practices, such as child abuse. Mystification is masking one's own interest by expressing it as if it were really to the advantage of someone else. For example, a parent may say to a child, "I'm sure you are tired and want to go to bed now," when the parent is the one who is exhausted and wants rest and privacy.[8]

Perhaps this all too brief introduction to family-systems theory can now help us be aware of what happens in remarriage; two separate family systems come together. The most usual process is that a man and a woman, each with a family system, are attracted to each other. They first attempt to relate to each other's family system. In time they marry. Then they try to have their whole family system relate to the other's whole family system. Each family has its own rules, roles, rituals, secrets, ghosts, mystification, and more. Each family's system differs from the other.

But they come together. They attempt to become a new family system, with each of the spouse's former families becoming a subsystem within that new family system. And this new family system must relate to a "suprasystem"—that is, all of the in-laws, former in-laws, former spouses, former spouses' spouses and children, and so forth.

While this may seem to be making the picture too complicated, it does provide a helpful way for family therapists (and the family itself) to ask, "What's going on here? Where is this family succeeding? Where is it experiencing difficulty? Where is the family experiencing different results than they hoped? How can this be changed and influenced?"

In short, family-systems theory lays bare how complex the task of building a remarried-family system is. It also provides a tool for identifying those areas and processes that need help and attention.

Problem Four: The New Family's Space, the Individual's Space, and the Couple's Space Must Be Defined

Another question the new stepfamily faces is this: "Where will we live?" This is a doubly important question for the new family. It has to do with finding the most comfortable home for the family and also involves powerful symbols. These symbols may be negative or positive. If a new partner, possibly with children, moves into a person's house, it may feel like invasion or intrusion. And those who move in may feel like unwelcome guests. If it is feasible for the family to find a new home, then decisions about the home and the use of space within that home can be a part of a family's new beginnings.

A man who had been living alone in his two-bedroom home married a woman who had a daughter, and they moved in with him. Because he had been using the second bedroom for a den, it was filled with expensive furniture, a beautiful desk, and a lovely bookcase full of treasured antique books. When his wife and stepdaughter moved in, he gave the stepdaughter his den for her bedroom. He moved his den furniture to the front room, except for the bookshelf full of books. "This is your room," he told her. For the daughter, however, the room didn't feel like her own; the bookshelf and books constantly reminded her that the room was not really hers and that she could not do what she liked with it. The new stepfather winced when he saw pictures of rock stars taped to the room's lovely walls. Even though he had had the best intentions, he felt as if his space was being invaded and his stepdaughter felt like an unwanted intruder.

The experiences of a number of people with whom we talked make it clear that obtaining a new home that all members of the family move into at the same time can provide an important opportunity for new beginnings and building a family structure. Beginnings tend to be more troubled when they take place in either of the previous homes.

And yet, there is room for variety here as well. One couple with whom we visited chose a different way. The husband offered to buy a different home with his new wife. (He was divorced and had custody of his three children; she was previously unmarried.) She considered the alternatives, and though glad to have been given the option, she chose to move into his existing home. They had a very definite plan, however. As money became available, they would transform that home and make it expressive of *her* tastes and creativity. They began by buying new bedroom furniture. Gradually, furnishings, decor, and yard have been transformed by the new family unit to be an expression of their new life together.

The decision on where to live involves a closely related issue: How do we make space (in a physical sense, but also in more than a physical sense) for individual, couple, and family needs? How does the married couple provide for couple needs? One couple answered this by selecting for themselves the most private, spacious bedroom in their new home. In this room they established a private conversation area. Then they equipped the room with a lock and announced to their children that there were times when they needed to be alone with each other, times that were definitely scheduled. They also notified family members always to knock before entering the bedroom. In this way, they clearly communicated their commitment to each other as a couple. They affirmed their enjoyment of each other and their resolve to maintain themselves as a couple in the face of any possible problems or threats.

The personal privacy needs of both adults and children in the household need to be discussed. Provisions for persons who need to be alone should be mutually agreed upon.

Because both partners in a remarriage probably had a home with furnishings and belongings, creating one home for the new family may be filled with conflicts and compromises. This is particularly true for widowed remarrying persons because they have all their possessions. Divorced persons probably divided theirs in the property settlement. However, successful remarried people point out that a strategy must be worked out so that the home is comfortable for all, expressive of all, and symbolic of a new family that has not forgotten its varied past-family heritages.

Problem Five: Complex Structure of Stepfamilies Requires Negotiating Skills

There is a wider involvement with more people in stepfamilies. Therefore, more people influence the family; any one individual has less control and has greater need of negotiating skills than in a first marriage.

When coauthor Carole recently went into a bank, she said to the official, "I'm Carole Della Pia-Terry, and I'd like to open a new account here." The bank official responded to her name by saying, "That sounds more like a corporation than a person!" Unwittingly, he had touched on a basic fact of remarriage; a lot of people are involved.

Said one man about the woman he loved, a divorcée with children and responsibilities to other people, "I realized she came as a package. I didn't comprehend the size of the package."[9]

As another man put it,

I didn't marry my wife, I married a crowd. . . . There are my three sons, who give me the silent treatment when they see me every other weekend, *and* the twin ten-year-old daughters of my new wife, Carolyn, who frankly are often a pain . . . *and* my new in-laws, who cold-shoulder me, *and* Carolyn's ex-husband, who spoils the kids rotten when he sees them, *and* my ex-wife, who is still bad-mouthing me to my kids, *and* the Bank of America's Credit and Loan Department.[10]

As Carole puts it, "There are thirty-one people who own a piece of me. And those are just the main ones. There are many more minor characters in this family structure." (See her family network chart.)

While in original families everyone is pretty clear about where the family boundary is—the family is everyone who lives at home—for the stepfamily the family boundaries are often confused and hazy. Some stepfamilies see in-laws, ex-in-laws, former spouses, and so forth, as part of some kind of extended family. Generally, however, most stepfamilies consider that two separate families overlap through the children. While not all members of the family belong to two families, the children do.[11]

The fact that the children maintain a relationship with both households, and probably spend some time in both, requires that the adults of both households deal with each other on a variety of matters: schedules, holidays, finances, and decisions concerning each child's welfare (medical, educational, recreational, and enrichment). But by far the most crucial matter that needs to be worked out among the adults is their input and involvement in the life of the children. Two sets of parents may have quite different standards, values, and styles in dealing with the children, and these should at least be understood. If the adults, including two persons who have divorced each other, still harbor anger or resentment, they can unfortunately see each other as enemies and, perhaps unconsciously, cast the children in the role of spies.[12]

For example, Virginia Satir tells of working with a sixteen-year-old girl who was alternately depressed and hyperactive. As Satir unraveled her situation, this is what she found. The girl lived with her mother and stepfather. One weekend a month, she visited her father and his fiancée; the next weekend she stayed with her father's previous wife and her new husband. The third weekend she spent with her maternal grandparents and the fourth weekend with her paternal grandparents. At each stop, she was pumped for information about what was going on in other places but was sworn to secrecy not to tell what was happening "here." Satir points out that the sad part was that all of these adults genuinely cared about the girl and wanted to help her, but unwittingly, they had put on her the burden for all the jealousy, rivalries, and resentments they harbored toward one another. When a therapist was able to confront these families with what they were doing, they were able to ease the situation by dealing with their own problems and not asking a sixteen-year-old girl to do so. As the girl very slowly and gradually learned to trust again, she no longer needed to be depressed or hyperactive.[13]

Even though former spouses probably do not go on loving each other,

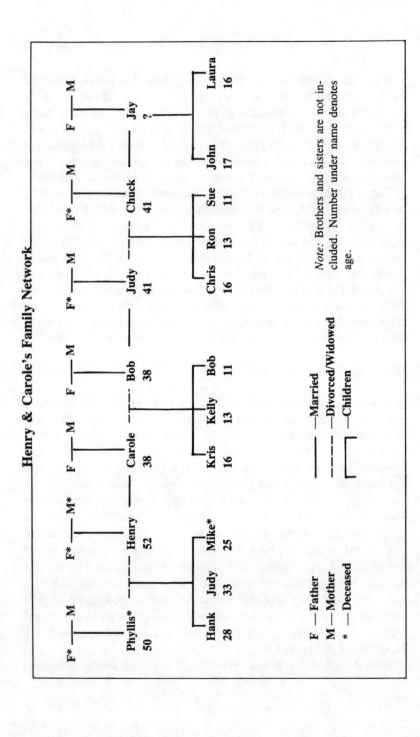

Henry & Carole's Family Network

they can be open and honest and not foist their problems with each other on their children. [14]

Widowed remarried persons with children will have a different situation. The need in this case is for maintaining contact between the dead person's family and the children and widowed spouse. For this extended family it would be an added grief to lose grandchildren and a son- or daughter-in-law after losing a child. And so we can see that, widowed or divorced, the remarried person may have a vast network of people who have some needs or expectations of him or her.

Problem Six: The Members of a Stepfamily May Not Stay Constant

The members of the family present in the household do not stay constant. They come and go.

Children for which a parent has custody may regularly spend weekends or vacations with another parent. Children for whom another parent has prime responsibility may arrive for short visits or extended vacation periods. One parent in such a family structure ruefully suggested that they would have planned better by putting a revolving door in their house!

These changes in the family make-up may have a fairly regular rhythm or may change rather drastically from time to time. The relocation of one parent due to a work obligation or opportunity may destroy the balance and may force all sorts of new decisions. For example, in one family the children visited their father on a regular basis *until* the family with primary custody was transferred two hundred miles away. After much discussion, the oldest daughter decided to live with her father and stepmother for a year, so that she could finish junior high school in her old home town. Then she rejoined her mother, stepfather, and siblings for her senior high years.

Parents in intact families experience some fairly rocky moments when dealing with maturing children. As children grow older, they want more privileges and freedom, while the parents ask them to take more responsibility. This transition from childhood to adolescence is often difficult when the children live with their parents. But when a parent says good-bye to her junior high "child" and then a year later resumes parenting her senior high "young adult," the subtleties of parenting are apt to be all the more delicate.

Studies show that it is important that a child have contact with both biological parents. The child's knowledge that both parents care about him or her is helpful to the child's search for identity. The child derives benefits from keeping in contact with both biological parents that are well worth the effort needed to make this happen.

Still, such an arrangement does have emotional costs for the child, and thus it will have an impact on the family as well. The visits back and forth vividly remind the child that he or she cannot be with all the persons he or she holds dear, at the same time. The child may secretly nourish the dream of getting his or her mother and father back together, but this dream gradually fades. Instead, the child finally realizes that the persons he or she loves are in different locations, live different lives, and cannot be brought together. As eleven-year-old Bob said, "I like to go see my dad, but I always feel sad when it's time to leave."

Children who move between two families probably experience variations in the standards of conduct expected by the adults in their lives. Methods of discipline are apt to become vague and ill-defined, and the children may feel confused.

A child may struggle with another issue, which is perhaps unspoken. "I'm not here all the time. Do I really belong here? Am I part of this family?" One suggestion for dealing with this is to provide space for each person who is part of your household family from time to time. In essence you say to the child, "Here's some closet space, a few hooks, a shelf, and a couple drawers that are all yours. Leave here what you would like to leave. You are part of us, and we look forward to your return."

Although this changing family scene may be stressful for all involved, it has its rewards as well. The child has the opportunity to relate to a number of adult models and also to see two adult couples relating to each other and to family. The child can share the interests of a number of parental adults and thus be exposed to new interests that he or she would not have been exposed to otherwise. The child may enjoy feeling the support of a number of adults when he or she performs in concerts, plays, athletic events, and so forth. As teenage Kristin said to her mother, "Mom, I have a lot of people loving me."

How Does a Couple Deal with This Complicated Structure in Which They Find Themselves?

A couple might begin to deal with the complicated structure of a step-family simply by recognizing the fact that structural issues will cause some stress in their lives. Carole recalls, "Early in my remarriage a lot of these things were going wrong, and I wondered what was wrong with me. An older remarried counselor and friend told me, 'It's not you, Carole. The system's against you.'" That much recognition can help, for it is the unrecognized, unseen forces in our lives that wreak the most havoc.

A couple might ask, "What is this family structure of which we are a part—at least, what are the elements of it we can see? What family systems are coming together?" Then they go on to ask what specific steps they can take to improve the quality of life within such a structure. Virginia Satir makes an important affirmation at this point, and her final caution is a good place to start:

> I believe in love—in loving and in being loved. I think that heterosexual love is the most rewarding and fulfilling feeling any human being can experience. Without loving and being loved, the human soul and spirit curdle and die. But love cannot carry all the demands of life. . . . Intelligence, information, awareness, and competence have to be added as well.[15]

Although Satir was speaking primarily of a couple building their relationship, the insight of her last statement applies also to building a family life, and especially to building family life in remarriage. Love is great; sex is great. But love and sex will not do all that needs to be done. The couple also need to pay attention to process, to structure, to the system.

In the light of this, a remarried couple may need to organize their use of time very carefully:

—There should be times when a parent spends time with his or her biological children, either as a group or as individuals. These children need to know that that parent-child relationship survives intact in the new marriage.

—There should be times when a stepparent spends time with his or her stepchildren, together and one on one. In this way the stepparent can build person-to-person relationships with the children.

—There should be times when both adults and children in the household plan to do things together. However, adults should not be surprised or offended if teenage children sometimes choose not to participate. In all families teenage children are in a process of separating themselves from their families.

—There should be couple time! (More on that later.)

Persons in complex stepfamily structures can claim their Christian resources to give them strength to live interdependently. The writer to Ephesians counsels us, "Therefore, putting away falsehood, let everyone speak the truth with his neighbor, *for we are members one of another"* (Ephesians 4:25, RSV, emphasis added). We are members, one of another. What a vivid description of those bound together in an extended remarried-family network! Christians should try to see this fact with eyes of faith as well, to see the other persons in the family as children of God, bound together in history and sharing concern for the children.

One woman (she was formerly single and married a divorced man) told us, "Early in our marriage, my husband's former wife was having a difficult time with their two boys. For quite some time, my husband found it necessary to be at her house helping with those boys every day. I didn't like it, for I would rather have had him home with me. I don't want to sound super-pious, but I do believe in prayer. And so I prayed—for my husband, for his two boys, for his former wife, and for me. And it's worked out. We all have a rather good relationship with each other now. But it would not have been so, if I had not passed that test early in our marriage."

We believe that persons with spiritual resources may face the difficult task of dealing with remarried family structure with hope, for "We are members one of another."

"We are members one of another."

"We are members . . . .

Questions for Reflection

1. Diagram your family network. See page 72 for an example.
2. What problems have you encountered because our society is vague about how people in a remarried family should act? For example:
   —inadequate names or terms for people in your system
   —lack of legal support for stepfamilies
   —lack of customs and conventions of family life
3. List the different family experiences in your new, remarried family. Which family experiences have had the most powerful influences? What special problems have you encountered (traditions, food, loyalty, etc.)?
4. What are some of the issues you deal with in your special family network?
5. What are the differences in the household rules, etc., that your children and stepchildren must deal with? How can you make the transition between their homes more tolerable?

7

Remarried Persons and Their Children

Family structure in remarriage is complicated. How then does the remarried couple deal with the children (hers and his) so that a workable family life with concern for the welfare of all members can be built?

The Starting Point in Dealing with Children of Remarriages

Where does the couple start? The couple starts by affirming and strengthening their own relationship. The couple must maintain an enriching and cohesive bond if each partner in the couple is to deal with the intense decisions and problems of the stepfamily.

In the midst of the stress and turmoil of building stepfamily relationships, the couple needs to preserve good communication. Many of the interactions may be heated and painful.

Partners must not give into the temptation to criticize and withdraw. Emotional sharing around parenting issues can build closeness because of the frequent need to deal with meaningful and urgent situations. The couple relationship will require constant attention, and if it develops through the challenge of stepparenting, the bonds will be strong and warmly felt.[1] The couple may need group discussions, group support, counseling, or therapy to maintain this strong couple bond during the challenges they face.

The couple start with the recognition that their relationship is the base on which their family life will be built. They choose each other, build a relationship with each other, and commit to each other because they believe that this shared life will be the most mutually enriching choice for the rest of their lives. Because they cherish their life together, they seek the strength to help them deal with the issues and stress that will come to it. They do not ignore the fact that either or both have children who will want and need attention, but they do affirm the primacy of their commitment to each other.

They agree that from the beginning they will take steps to nurture their couple relationship. If they need time alone weekly, they will take steps to get it. They agree that they hope to build bonds with each other that will be satisfying as their bonds with their maturing children diminish. They expect to be together after the children are launched into their own independent lives.

They also agree (this is the most important part) that they will not let anything come between them. They will strive to talk to each other about anything—even about each other's children. While it is too much to expect that they will always agree, they will keep talking and not cut each other off even when they disagree.

The couple know that their primary commitment to each other will ultimately work to the benefit of their children. Of course, their couple commitment will be challenged. Quite likely, the first challenge will come from children. Either partner in the couple who has children by a previous marriage may have a close bond with those children.

Children who have a strong bond with a parent may want to be consulted before their parent remarries, and they may want to approve the choice. While couples should be sensitive to the children's needs and include them in discussions of how they will fit into the new arrangement, the decision to remarry and form this new couple bond is the adults' decision.

Balancing this strong (and long) relationship to one's children with a strong (but briefer) relationship to a new spouse is a delicate task. Virginia Satir comments that people seem to relate in triangles. That is, when three people are interacting, two relate directly and the third is left out. The third person can choose how to respond to that; she or he can either simply observe what is going on with the other two and support it, or raise an objection that she or he is left out.[2] If both one's children and one's new spouse clamor that they feel left out of this triangle, it changes from a triangle to a tug of war. The person in the middle might feel wanted by both parties but is much more likely to feel stretched like a piece of rope. The tension is resolved when both parties feel that they have their own place and that they are receiving appropriate attention and care. But the potential for conflict and rivalry will be there at all times.

Example: In a family that was making a rather good adjustment to remarriage, a man told his stepson Jack, "Remember our family rule. No more than fifteen minutes on the phone. You've been talking for fifteen minutes. Get off the phone." "I haven't been on for fifteen minutes," Jack objected. "Yes, you have. Get off the phone." Jack grudgingly did so and said nothing more until his mother came home. Then he blurted out to her, "Your husband called me a liar." The wife angrily attacked her husband. Only after considerable discussion was the event reported accurately and calm restored to the house. In a moment of tension the bond to child felt much stronger than the bond to husband.

Example: A stepfather was disciplining his six-year-old stepson for what he considered "babyish" behavior. The mother observed briefly; then she could take no more and shouted, "He's my kid, and I'll take care of him!" The mother confided later that she values the stepfather's modeling of what it means to be a man to her son but feels unable to accept his discipline of her son, which she feels is sometimes too harsh. Her message to her husband is this: my relationship to my son is not a part of my life that I am willing to share with you.

A couple need to deal with each other about their children for the children's sakes as well as for their own. One person with whom we visited shared this experience as she looked back on the beginning of her remarried family life. "Ben (her second husband) and I had a hard summer in 1972 when we were first married. Ben's sixteen-year-old son was testing the limits in this new family. I was resentful that Ben didn't say anything or do anything. This was hard for me (and for him also, I found out later). My son Louis, who was twenty-one, was living with us that summer. So I turned to Louis, the only remnant of our old comfy family life, in which the rules had been different (much more restrictive and defined). I turned to Louis with my anger, discomfort, and disbelief. I wanted his pat on the back to let me know that I was 'right,' that Ben was out of line and Ben's sixteen-year-old son was getting away with murder. Even then I could sense Louis's discomfort at being used as my problem solver. This should not have been his role. Many years later, he was still working through his anger, not at Ben or Ben's son, but at me, for *using* him. He couldn't have had the wisdom to settle anything at that point. More than that, he was trying to learn to love his new stepfather, and he appreciated the stability and wholeness Ben gave to us all. It would have been much better for me to find a sympathetic friend or counselor to help me find ways of dealing with the chaos of those early testing months. My talking, ridiculing, blaming, and complaining would have best been done with Ben himself. Anyway, we survived, somehow. The strong 'goods' in our life—good sex, good humor, good income, two good strong professions—helped us go on to happier times. (Incidently, we were both widowed, so there were no other spouses to bring into this.)"

There is one caution to add here. We are not saying that the newly remarried couple should become so wrapped up in each other that they are unaware of their own children's feelings and needs. We are not saying that they should "tune the children out." Indeed, that may be a problem early in remarriages. What we are saying is the the partners should build couple strength and nurture that strength to face the many challenges that will come from the puzzling process of parenting and stepparenting.

And so, we repeat that the place to begin is with the couple's commitment to a strong relationship with each other. As one woman with whom we visited advised, "Take time for yourselves. Go back to ground zero, just the two of you. Talk about everything in your lives together." Build understanding. Build togetherness. Build love.

Deciding What to Call Family Members

One of the first things a new family formed by remarriage need to discuss is this: What will we call each other? If the children are small, perhaps they will simply be told; but if the children are older, they may want to enter into the discussion and decision.

What should the children be called? That's the easiest part, probably; they are simply called by their names. But how does the stepparent introduce a stepchild? "This is my stepson, Bob?" "This is my son, Bob?" "This is my boy, Bob?" What would the child prefer?

The question of what to call a stepparent is more difficult. Perhaps the children used a name before the remarriage: George, or Uncle George, or Mr. Edwards. Perhaps in the early stages of the remarriage, they'd like to retain the use of that name until they feel more comfortable in the new family relationship and structure. What would the stepparent like to be called? What would the children like? If the stepparent has biological children, how do they feel about what their stepsiblings call their father or mother?

Carole and her daughter Kelly were once talking to a neighbor and little boy. Kelly knew the family had a stepson and natural son. Kelly turned to the little boy and asked, "Is that your *real* Dad?" Kelly in her naive way was trying to decide who had what role in the boy's family. Not knowing what to call the father, she had qualified the term with the word "real."

Some people feel that if children use first names for that stepparent, this implies decreased authority for that adult. Others see authority and naming as two separate issues.

The wisdom of those who see the naming issue most clearly is this: don't ever violate children's emotional space by insisting that they call a stepparent "Mother" or "Father" before they are ready to do so. (The adult stepparent may also be aware of emotional space needs and not want to be called "Mother" or "Father" before she or he feels ready.) Once the child feels ready and senses that this is no betrayal of the natural parent, the child may call two women "Mother" and two men "Father." Never mind the confusion; the child knows which parent he or she means!

Co-author Carole and her husband, Henry, note that Carole's children call Henry "Dad" until they are around their biological father; then they call him "Henry." This seems to represent some sensitivity to their biological father's feelings.

Because names and titles are symbols of evolving relationships and roles, early decisions need to be made about what to call each other. But it should be clearly stated that this is an open-ended conversation that may be reopened at any time.

Relationship of Stepparents to Stepchildren

How do stepparents feel about their stepchildren? How do the stepchildren feel about their stepparents? How should they relate?

Many folks tell us that frequently children do not view the remarriage with the same enthusiasm that the adults do.

Children may secretly feel that the break-up of their parents' original marriage was their fault. Therefore, they may be anxious for their parents to get back together. A remarriage would prevent that. Once the break-up has occurred, the child may enjoy a particularly close bond in that single parent family. The child may be given leadership and responsibility in the one-parent family, which is much enjoyed. But when the child sees an adult coming in as a replacement, taking the child's place as the person closest to the parent, she or he may feel overwhelmed with the change. Quite likely, the child will take out this uneasiness and resistance on the stepparent. The child may choose to ignore the stepparent or refuse any suggestions or overtures of friendship from the stepparent. She or he may be sullen and disrespectful and may not even try to disguise a strong feeling of resentment for the invader.

This behavior may simply be a response to the general discomfort that change brings, or it may be much more purposeful. The child may be unable to let go of that secret fantasy that his or her parents will get back together again. The child may even hold onto this fantasy after both parents have remarried. In fact, part of the child's strategy may be to disrupt and destroy each parent's present marriage so that his or her parents can marry each other again.

Person after person among the remarried persons we interviewed told us that they sensed resistance from their children and stepchildren. It was a rare exception when this did not happen. Sometimes the resistance lasted for years.

What did those who successfully dealt with this resistance do? For one thing, they gave the anger an opportunity to heal. With an understanding of the source of this anger, stepparents can steel themselves against the hurt and avoid responding in kind. And then, maybe the stepparents can help talk it out; for example,

"You're not my father. I hate you."
"I hear you. We still have to live together. You are angry with me. You miss your dad? It must be hard. Are you angry with him?"[3]

For another thing, the adults can be firm and clear about the way things will be. A man who brought his two teenage daughters with him into a remarriage found himself annoyed at the hurtful way they responded to his new wife, Ann. He firmly and repeatedly told them, "Ann and I are married and we intend to stay that way. That's the way it is. If you want to be part of this family, you are welcome to stay. But the fact of our marriage is not going to change. You will either need to accept it or find some other living situation where you will be happier." Now he is happy to report that with time, firmness, and patience, his daughters have become rather good friends with their stepmother.

But the stepchild may be dealing with another problem: confusion about loyalty. The child may feel that it is disloyal to the biological parent to like or even love the stepparent. This is true whether the absent biological parent is dead or alive. Even the kindest, gentlest, most caring stepparent may create emotional turmoil in the child. The child may feel drawn to this kindness and yet not be sure that it is OK to respond with love and kindness.

To deal with this confusion in her own children, Carole shared with them the image of the cookie jar and the water spigot. It went something like this. "Some people think that love is like a cookie jar. There are just so many cookies in the jar and when you use them all up, they're gone. Actually, love is more like the water in the spigot. Whenever you go to the spigot, the water is there—all you need. And so if you are thinking of love as a cookie jar, you may be worried that you don't have enough "love cookies" to go around to all your parents. You're afraid that if you love your father and me, you won't have enough love to give to your stepmother and your stepfather. But don't worry. Your love is like the water in the spigot. There's plenty of love to give your dad and your stepmother, Henry, your stepfather, and me." In so doing, Carole vividly and clearly gave her children permission and freedom to love all of the adults in their lives without feeling conflict or disloyalty.

The stepchild, however, is not the only one who has feelings with which to deal. The stepparent also must cope with feelings. The person who enters the remarriage family expecting that "because I love you, I will love your children; it will be easy, simple, and natural" will have a rude awakening. That is an unrealistic expectation, at least at first.

Esther Wald points out that when children are born into a nuclear family, the couple share four ties to the children, biological, legal, developmental, and social (family life together). When a couple divorces, the absent parent retains the biological and legal ties, but loses the others. The single parent retains all four ties to the children. When the single parent remarries, the absent parent still retains the biological and legal ties to the children. The new spouse has no ties to the children except the founding of a new social unit, the new remarried family. In time that new stepfamily will contribute to the developmental tie between children and adult. But as the remarriage begins, all the new spouse and the stepchildren have in common is a bond to a person important to both of them.[4] This, then, is the more realistic starting point: the new stepparent and the new stepchildren have in common a person they both care about; they share common living arrangements and a reason to try to become friends. Because both the children and the adults have a lot to work out, this process may be slow and difficult.

One remarried woman whom we interviewed recalled the early days of her second marriage. "Before this marriage, I had never had people who didn't like me. But my new husband's kids did not like me at all, and my husband, who wanted to please everybody, was caught in the middle. Everybody was not going to be pleased! We went to some family therapy, just four sessions or so, and eventually we broke through to each other. But it took time. I remember a vacation trip we took together. There was a lot of discord, sullenness, and rudeness. Finally, I had had enough. I told those kids, 'I withdraw my energy from you. I choose to quit trying so hard with you. I still care for you, but I am not going to beat my head against a wall any longer.' Strangely enough, when they heard how I felt and when I quit trying so hard, things improved a little.''

That stepmother was discovering what Emily and John Visher counsel:

> Caring relationships take time to evolve. The expectation of "instant love" between stepparents and stepchildren can lead to many disappointments and difficulties. If the stepfamily relationships are allowed to develop as seems comfortable to the individuals involved, then caring between step-relatives has the opportunity to develop.[5]

Stepparents also need to be clear about the distinction between *feelings* and *behavior* with their stepchildren. It was with considerable wisdom that a woman who has both natural children and stepchildren in the same household spoke, saying, "I don't feel the same about all these children. After all I bore, diapered, and suffered through infant diseases with some, but not with all. Those experiences formed a bond with my children that is deep and vital. I cannot deny it exists. I can't create it where it doesn't exist. I no longer feel guilty about it. I feel differently about my stepchildren. But I give to all—children and stepchildren—fair discipline, caring parenting. I can't *feel* the same, but I can *do* practically the same for them.''

And this brings us to the next topic.

Discipline

What about discipline? Who should do it? When? How? What do we do if one of the children really gets into trouble?

Lucile Duberman uses the term "parent work" to mean those essential tasks that parents (or stepparents) must perform to aid their children grow to successful maturity. The six are:

1. *maintenance*—parents must provide for the survival of their children by seeing to it that they have food, shelter, clothing, and physical care;

2. *guidance* or *socialization*—parents must provide moral teaching and transmit the values, beliefs, and goals of the society;

3. *discipline*—parents must apply limits in order to teach self-restraint and compliance with behavioral norms and standards;

4. *assistance*—parents must help children to grow up and cope with life situations (assistance may take the form of advice, instruction and/or financial help);

5. *love* and *respect*—parents must relate to children so that the children believe in their own self-worth (the children are not to be treated as objects to be manipulated nor as inferior beings to be exploited, but as people with feelings and rights);

6. *release*—parents must let the children go when it is right for them to leave the family home (parents are expected to train their children to be independent and to help them separate themselves from the nuclear family when they mature enough to do so).[6]

Duberman used this list to evaluate the performance of the stepparents that she had studied. She felt that the areas of discipline, advice, and socialization were the weakest areas; most of the leadership in these areas was left in the hands of the stepchild's biological residential parent. She noted that when the child was visiting in the home of the parent and stepparent who did not have custody, the adults often chose not to enforce any discipline. Rather, they used the time for recreation, love, and strengthening the relationship. Stepparents who lived with their spouse's children often saw that spouse as too lenient and as not disciplining the children sufficiently. The stepparents often did not feel that they had the right to discipline the children even if they thought the children needed it. Some stepparents who had begun to participate in the discipline of children felt that they had received clear messages (from both spouse and stepchildren) that their involvement was not wanted. So they drew back.[7]

This is what one observer called the "eggshell phenomenon." That is, some stepparents are afraid to discipline the stepchild because they fear the reaction of their mate. Instead, they "walk on eggshells" and avoid disciplining the child, fearing both the child's reaction to the "wicked stepparent'' and the spouse's words, "You can't tell my child what to do!'' Some stepparents even worry that if they cannot get along with the children all of the time, their spouse might leave them.[8]

The remedy for the "eggshell phenomenon" is for the couple to sit down together, away from distractions, and discuss discipline. They might share their ideas about the goals of discipline, the methods to use, and the ways to support one another in disciplinary situations. The couple might want to make two lists independently of each other. One list would be of the nonnegotiable areas in which the child has no say in the decision making; the parents have full control. The other list is of the negotiable matters in which the child has some choice in the decision making. Once parent and stepparent have compared their lists, discussed them, and agreed upon them, then, together, they should present the lists to the child. The biological parent needs to let the child know that this is what is expected and that the stepparent has the parent's full permission to discipline.[9]

Some couples get this far in building a mutual disciplinary style but then find that it breaks down in day-to-day living. One couple described the tensions they felt in discipline. She (the biological parent) said: "It's nice to have his firm hand in raising the children, but sometimes the firm hand gets a little too heavy. I think he comes down too hard on the kids at times, and then I interfere to get him to ease off.'' He (the stepparent) said: "We seem to agree on the main items of discipline, but disagree on dozens of details. One of us will contradict the other before the children. It's no wonder the kids are confused.''

Another couple, who had made a little more progress in the area of discipline, had decided on this strategy: even when they disagreed with what the other did in discipline (or did not do in discipline), they would never contradict each other in front of the children. They would make a point to bring up the incident and discuss it privately. If a child asked for a decision about which they were uncertain, they asked the child to leave the room so they could discuss it before they gave the child an answer. They still had tensions in disciplining because no two adults approach discipline in exactly the same way. But they did reduce the discipline tension to manageable size.

Of course, when a remarriage is new, discipline does not start on this nearly equal, partnership basis. Children, after all, have little interest in responding to discipline until they feel a friendly relationship and rapport with an adult whom they have accepted as part of the household. This often takes one and a half to two years. This period of nurturing friendship must occur before the stepparent enters heavily into sharing the discipline. However, from the outset the adults can support each other's authority in the household. The biological parent can make clear that when he or she is not present, the stepparent will have authority to see that family rules are carried out (after all, such authority is given even to a baby-sitter).

The wisest course for new stepparents seems to be for them to ease into the parenting role. They need to get the feel of how the family operates; see its strengths and weaknesses; privately discuss with their spouses what seems most in need of change. Spouses need to be very sensitive to and supporting of each other, making a few changes slowly. The family cannot be reformed overnight.

The purpose of discipline is the growth and learning of the child. Sometimes adults let other agendas slip into disciplining. Perhaps their frustration or anger slips in. Troubles with their former or present spouse may be expressed in harsher discipline of the child. Persons should be sensitive to these possibilities and avoid them if at all possible.

When the adults and children have built a sturdy remarriage family together, several different styles of discipline may evolve.

—In one couple we observed, each parent has virtually total responsibility for disciplining his or her biological children. The other adult, however, serves as "consultant" to the biological parent, so that this parent does not feel alone in the difficult decisions of parenting.

—In some couples we observed, the stepparent was fully absorbed. The stepparent entered into and enforced discipline decisions with a shared authority with the biological parent that was seldom questioned.

—In some couples, the biological parent clearly has the decision-making power about his or her children, but the stepparent has the authority to interpret and enforce those decisions in the absence of the parent.

—In still another style, which we read about but did not observe, the two adults locate areas of behavior in their children and stepchildren that are important to one parent and not to the other. They then agree that the parent to whom the area is important has the responsibility for seeing that his or her principles are upheld; the other spouse will not interfere. For example, if it is important to one parent that the son's hair be cut once a month (and the other parent does not really care), the parent to whom it is important should be in charge of taking the boy to the barbershop and dealing with his resistance or complaints. The other parent does not interfere. [10]

We have been saying that a stepparent's first task is to develop a friendly, caring, and nurturing atmosphere—to the extent possible in the face of resistance—with the children. Then biological parent and stepparent should gradually enter into a mutually agreed upon, mutually supportive discipline plan that fits them and, according to the couple's best lights, contributes to each child's growth and maturing.

While it takes time for the newly remarried couple to work out their child-rearing style, it is important to come to a mutual, collaborative style as early as possible. Laura Singer points out, ". . . as you and the children mature, unresolved problems tend to grow as well." [11] In adolescent years, these unresolved problems may become more dramatic and divisive for parents. Unresolved disagreements about child rearing can surface again with new accusations such as, " 'If only you'd made him do his homework and respect authority years ago, he wouldn't be a dropout today, bumming around the country, stoned on grass.' 'What do you mean? if *you* hadn't been so harsh, he wouldn't have wanted to strike back and rebel. He ran from that kind of life you showed him.' " [12]

There are many different ways to raise children to be relatively wholesome and positive people. The basic factor, however, is that the home be a place where the adult parent figures have worked through their feelings about each other and about the child-raising process so that they can avoid expressing their inner conflicts through interaction with the children. [13]

Occasionally, an adolescent child will get into serious trouble. This is not only upsetting to the child but also extremely disruptive to the couple and to family harmony. Whatever the difficulty, the parental figures will likely respond, (a) "What, our child?" (b) "It's my fault; I shouldn't have. . . ." (c) "It's your fault; you shouldn't have. . . ."

When a child is in difficulty, the first parental responses are almost always to blame oneself and then to blame one's partner. But parents need to move beyond that. They need to discover within themselves the compassion to forgive both themselves and their partners for mistakes they may have made. (The child's difficulty, however, may not be a sign of any particular parental mistakes.) After forgiveness and compassion take over in their attitudes toward selves, each other, and the child, "only then can the child's behavior be examined and understood, the relationship between spouses explored and strengthened, and perhaps the interaction between parents and child restructured.''[14]

The Effect of the Ages of the Children on Coparenting Style

Do the ages of the children at the time we begin the remarriage influence how we begin coparenting? If so, how?

The ages of the children at the time of the remarriage will certainly affect the couple's strategy for developing cooperative parenting and disciplining. Because *preschool children* have less history and memory about the previous marriage, they may enter into the new family most easily. Children this age react strongly to the feelings and behavior of the adults around them, and so the adults should share freely their excitement and hope for a good family life together.

Young children also have a need for routine, order, and predictability. Informing the child of routines and establishing them in the new family will be important. If the child visits in another parent's home, the plans and schedules should be clearly and simply shared with the child. For example, one couple allows the child to have her own calendar. They color in the days when she will visit the other parent, and they do what they can to make transitions for her predictable and as easy as possible.

Children six to twelve years old will have different needs when the newly remarried couple begin life with them. For one thing, they may feel guilt and anger over the termination of the former marriage, and they may have very mixed loyalties to both biological parents. Anger and conflict may frighten them. Particularly with children in this age group, it is important to assure them that when a parent is angry with them, the anger does not mean the parent does not love them. A parent needs to make clear that he or she is *not* going to divorce the child, that the child is there to stay. Children need to be reassured that it was not their behavior that caused the divorce. Children this age probably feel as though a tornado has struck their lives; they are desperate for stability. Predictability, reliability, promise keeping, and routine are important for them. The Vishers offer the following counsel in helping remarried parents begin a new life with children this age:

1. "Let them know you understand how upsetting it is to have so many changes about which they have no say going on in their lives." At the same time, the parents may have to help children with the behavior by which they express their emotions. Feelings and behavior are different.

Behavior must be controlled, but feelings do not have to be. They can be expressed and accepted even if they are extremely negative.

2. "Help your children find nondestructive ways to express the physical and emotional energy caused by angry feelings." Punching a punching bag or pillow, pounding nails, running, walking—these are some nondestructive ways children can express some of the turmoil going on inside.

3. "Give the children as many choices as possible for different aspects of their lives." For example, allow children free choice over what they want to wear, what they want to eat for breakfast or school lunch, how they spend their allowances or gift money, what friends they want to be with and so on. When a child is adjusting to many changes over which he or she has no control, a sense of mastery over as much as possible is important. [15]

Incidentally, some studies reveal that the stepfamily has a greater chance of successful adjustment if the oldest child is less than thirteen. [16]

Teenage children present other issues to the newly remarried couple attempting to integrate a stepfamily. Teenagers are in the process of breaking away from family bonds, searching for their independence and individuality. They are "trying their wings."

Teenagers are turning increasingly to their peers for advice, counsel, and support. When a recent marriage has occurred in their family, teenagers may turn even more quickly to peers and withdraw even more from the newly forming family. They will probably be more reluctant than younger brothers or sisters to become part of the new household. "As one sixteen-year-old said, 'Two parents are too many! I don't need still another adult telling me what to do!'" [17]

The remarried family that involves children who are adolescents at the time of the union probably need a specific strategy for dealing with them. For one thing, the couple may need to discuss their list of nonnegotiable items with the teenager, agreeing that in the foreseeable future the biological parent will enforce these whenever possible. They may want to plan how the stepparent can offer interest, help, and support to the teenager, an offer that may be rejected. Quite probably they will allow the teenage child to withdraw from much active participation in the household, leaving the door open so that the youth can return later as a young adult. When older teenagers leave home, it does not mean that they are disappearing forever! [18]

Dealing with Stepsibling Rivalry

How do we deal with stepsibling rivalry? Lucile Duberman explored stepsibling relationships in the remarried families she studied. She located at least four factors that seem to contribute to good stepsibling relationships: (a) the residence of the children; that is, the children live in the same house with each other, rather than simply seeing each other occasionally; (b) the remarried parents having a child or children together (this may be true, but there may be other factors to consider; parents should not have another child *just* to bring the family together, nor should they attempt this too soon, before the rest of the family has had time to jell); (c) a successful marital relationship between the stepparents; and (d) a good relationship between stepparents and stepchildren.[19]

Beyond consideration of these factors, what wisdom might be shared for dealing with stepsibling rivalries?

—Recognize that sibling rivalry is widespread and that stepsibling rivalry is to be expected. It may be frustrating or maddening at times, but it is probably quite normal.

—Agree on your nonnegotiable minimum, which some remarried couples state somewhat like this, "You don't have to love each other, but you do need to respect each other's needs and learn to live together. You can argue, but you can't hurt or abuse each other."

—Give children as much freedom as possible to work out stepsibling relationships. If rooms are to be shared, the children themselves may want to choose who shares what room. "As one girl put it, 'I could really like my stepsister because I was free to do it. No one said I *had* to like her.'"[20] Don't work too hard at promoting good relationships. A sense of pressure may go with that effort. You may have to negotiate conflict at times; you may even have to keep someone from hurting someone else. But how friendly they choose to be should be up to them. Here are some guidelines.

—As much as possible, don't have favorites.

—Don't hold up one child as an ideal or model for another child to follow, even if two children of similar age have marked differences between them.

—Allow each child his or her own uniqueness, interests, needs, and rate of growing up.

—If there are several stepsiblings coming together, it is quite normal for family life to be somewhat chaotic. Be patient; give them time. If they seem to have intense bitterness and hatred or if their conflicts seem to be locked in and are not being resolved, you may want to seek professional family counseling. But a fair amount of turbulence is normal.

—Provide for growing children's privacy needs. (See the next section.)

—Don't get "sucked into" taking sides with your biological children against your stepchildren (or vice versa). Keep abreast of this matter as a couple. Be aware of what tensions the stepsiblings may be causing in your couple relationship. Deal with that and approach the children with a united strategy.

Incest in Stepfamilies

Is it true that there is more incest in stepfamilies? What can we as parents do about it?

It is a known fact that "incest taboos" (society's clear prohibition of sex between family members) are weaker in stepfamilies. One should not engage in sexual activities with a brother or sister, but are stepsiblings brothers and sisters? One should not engage in sexual activity with one's mother or father, but is a stepparent really mother or father? The answers are confused, and thus we have one more area of tension with which to deal in the remarried family.

Although some persons who work with families and some studies indicate that incest occurs more frequently in remarried families, this is such a delicate matter that it is difficult to know how frequently. Dr. Lenore Terr sees incest as being much more than just sexual intercourse. In this broader definition, Dr. Terr has frequently seen incest between stepsiblings. Since they are not blood relatives, they are more likely to interact sexually. When they do this, however, they do not feel good about it. The uneasiness and guilt they feel over relating sexually to another "family" member can be harmful.[21]

In addition to unclear sexual taboos, another factor contributing to sexual interest and curiosity may be "the often highly erotic climate in the home as the new couple express their positive sexual feelings toward each other."[22] The touching, kissing, and fondling that the newly remarried couple do may have an unsettling erotic effect on children awakening to their own sexual desires and needs. One teenage stepdaughter put it bluntly, "'There I was with my own sex drives, and I wasn't getting anywhere.

Why should my mother, of all people, be getting hers with her new husband?'''[23]

Esther Wald cites the case of the Roberts family. Shortly after Mr. and Mrs. Roberts had been married, Mr. Roberts's son Stan, age sixteen, came to live with him, his new wife, and Mrs. Roberts's two daughters by a previous marriage. Tracy was also sixteen and her younger sister was twelve.

> Mr. and Mrs. Roberts were pleased that Tracy, her older daughter, appeared to take Stan over and include him in her activities. Indeed, they ruefully acknowledged that they were so involved in their own marital relationship they had not noticed how intense the relationship between Stan and Tracy had become. It was only while attending a school function that they learned that Tracy and Stan were considered boyfriend and girlfriend and not brother and sister. . . .
>
> When Mr. and Mrs. Roberts came to a local youth guidance clinic they were extremely agitated, angry, and frustrated. They had just learned that . . . Stan and . . . Tracy . . . were sexually active with each other.
>
> In their efforts to put an end to this relationship Mrs. Roberts felt that Stan should return to live with his mother; Mr. Roberts thought that Tracy should go to live with her grandmother. Both were outraged that the ''other's'' child should do this to ''his'' and to ''her'' child. Neither seemed willing to consider any other alternatives.[24]

Wald notes several factors that contributed to Stan's and Tracy's sexual involvement with each other: the heightened sexuality in the household because of the newness of the parents' remarriage; the ''stranger'' phenomenon—that is to say, Stan and Tracy had not grown up together; the lack of boundary setting; and the lack of an appropriately supervised environment in which they could build their relationship. After the involvement, there was no solid family base to help each young person move beyond the crisis. Instead each parent had become an ally to his or her own child and the accuser of his or her stepchild. This was a tragic, disruptive situation. It would have been much better to have dealt with this by anticipation and prevention.

Such intense sexual acting out may be fairly rare. But the presence of sexual awareness and sexual tension within the family will not be rare. One male, as he looked back on his experience of becoming a stepson in his early teens, recalls the sexual conflict he experienced:

''I was always thinking about girls and I was always thinking about sex. And one of my fantasy objects was my stepsister. This was particularly tough because I felt both attracted to women and afraid of women, and there she was in various states of undress. Whether she actually was or not, I really don't remember. I was attracted to her, and I was curious about her both as an individual and as a symbol. She was too close to ignore. I couldn't distance from her in that house.

"Another one of my objects was my stepmother. And that was even worse! It was even more threatening to me because I was attracted to her sexually and I went out to her emotionally, too. There was a lot there in my head. Really, my fear about my sexual feelings about my stepmother kept me from expressing some of my positive emotions toward her."[25]

So we see that sexual feelings and fantasies may be experienced both toward stepsiblings and stepparents.

One young man wrote his stepmother a passionate love letter from boarding school. Years later, he remembers his gratitude over the way she handled it. She recruited his father to join with her in writing a letter to him. The letter said how happy they both were that he had accepted her as stepmother, and that she was just as happy to have him as her new stepson. They wrote that they loved each other greatly, and his acceptance of their marriage meant a great deal to them. The young man set aside his romantic fantasies about his stepmother on the day he received that letter. He settled into the role of son. He did so with relief, but he never really knew whether his stepmother understood the intent of his letter. As he looks back, he sees a mature handling of a situation that could have had many unfortunate consequences if his stepmother had dealt with it in another fashion.[26]

What then should the wise couple do about the matter of incestuous feelings in their remarried family? They should be aware, anticipate, and create a setting in which the issue can be handled.

—Give guidelines by which the family will live. One couple we know set the ground rules that children will either wear bathrobes or be dressed when they're with each other. They will not go into each other's bedrooms without knocking. The children sometimes find this cumbersome and tell the adults that they are hung up on sex. But the parents are willing to endure this minor ridicule for the sake of providing what they feel is a safe, secure situation in which their similar-age children from two previous marriages can grow up together.

—Provide for adult presence. Do not have long periods of unsupervised absence.

—At the same time, don't overreact. Stepsiblings who grew up with each other from early childhood are apt to think of each other as brother and sister and probably need less of the structure and supervision we have described. Adolescent or preadolescent stepsiblings who come together as strangers have a greater need for such a protective atmosphere.

—From both your perspective and that of your children, recognize that sexuality is part of a person and does not just go away. Sexual feelings may be disguised in teasing, anger, flirting, or many other ways. All should recognize that, in this area as in any other, there is nothing wrong with the *feelings*. The *behavior*, on the other hand, needs to be channeled in appropriate ways.

—If the remarried couple's demonstrativeness creates an erotic atmosphere that may add to their children's discomfort, should they quit being affectionate in front of the children? No. The modeling of a loving relationship between a man and a woman is one of the good things they can share with their children. The couple will want to be sensitive, however, to the impact their behavior is having on their children and save their more erotic expressions for private times.

Faith Resources That Can Aid in the Development of a Reconstituted Family

The Bible makes quite clear that marriage and parenthood can be part of one's Christian calling. (So can being single.)

The Bible makes clear that all the guidance and power of the Christian faith directs us toward loving, sustaining communities of people. We see this in what the New Testament says about the church. In Ephesians 2, the writer recalls the great divisions that existed between Jews and non-Jews. But the writer proclaims that Christ broke down the dividing wall between them, and at the conclusion he writes, "So then, you Gentiles [non-Jews, outsiders] are not foreigners or strangers any longer; you are now fellow-citizens with God's people and members of the family of God" (Ephesians 2:19). The phrase used for church there is "family of God." Indeed, the church has a resemblance to a family, at least to a remarried family. In the church, a group of diverse people come together because they all have love for one person—Jesus Christ. In the remarried family, diverse people come together because they share love for a person. A stepfather and his stepchildren both share love for the woman who is his wife and their mother. For that reason they come together and attempt to build a loving community. When that family, in common, love yet another presence—God in Christ—they have an additional bond holding them together against all the strains that would tear them apart.

The New Testament speaks of those who share the Christian faith as "family." It also uses another term to suggest how people get into the family; it says a person comes in by adoption. For example, in Galatians Paul writes that God sent Christ

> . . . so that we might receive adoption as sons. And because you are sons, God has sent the Spirit of his Son into our hearts, crying, "Abba! Father!" So through God you are no longer a slave but a son, and if a son then an heir (Galatians 4:5b-7, RSV).

Quite clearly, the New Testament uses the term "adoption" as a symbol of incredible privilege. People who were slaves become sons and daughters, members of God's family, heirs of all that God intends for them. That image of adoption may be an important faith symbol for forming reconstituted families. True, formal legal adopting does not usually take place in such families. But a lot of informal "adopting" can happen, opening up a bright rich future for those involved. And the Christian faith affirms that it is so.

When the Bible gives guidance to parents on parenting (for example, Exphesians 6:4: "You fathers, again, must not goad your children to resentment, but give them the instruction, and the correction, which belong to a Christian upbringing" [NEB]), that instruction is not based on any biological bond. Rather, it is based on the importance and dignity of the child, and upon the tremendous value of that child's soul. These principles apply equally to stepfamilies and original families.

New Testament love is not the romantic outpouring of affection between man and woman nor the automatic bonding between a mother and child. Rather, it is the intentional act of loving others as God has loved us in Christ. The remarried family presents the new members a fresh opportunity to begin again in family life. It is a time to establish the goal that Christian love will be the mark of building the new family. It is an opportunity to see how closely the members of this family can approximate Paul's beautiful teachings.

Love has good manners and does not pursue selfish advantage. It is not touchy. It does not keep account of evil or gloat over the wickedness of other people. On the contrary, it is glad . . . when truth prevails. Love knows no limit to its endurance, no end to its trust, no fading of its hope . . . (1 Corinthians 13:5-7, Phillips).

So may it be in your new family.

Successful Parenting

Are we saying then, that in spite of the difficulties, successful parenting is possible in remarried families? Yes! Some parents-stepparents tell us that they did not find it nearly as difficult as we have described it. Many of those who have faced all we have said and more, still talk of the satisfaction of seeing sound, healthy children emerging in accepting, respecting, and sometimes even loving relationships with siblings, stepsiblings, and parental adults. We know stepfamilies can succeed because we know many that have.

Strengthened by their Christian faith, aware adults can create a caring atmosphere in which both children and adults will flourish. And, we repeat, we believe a strong family life will most likely happen when the couple build a bond between them that is so stable that they can deal with their own and their partner's children.

Questions for Reflection

1. What do the members of your remarried family call each other? Are these names acceptable to all involved?
2. Were your stepchildren resistent to having you as their new stepparent? How did you resolve this conflict?
3. Did you expect "instant love" between the stepparent and stepchildren in your remarried family? How were all of your true feelings dealt with?
4. How is discipline handled in your remarried family? Do you find any of the suggestions for discipline given in this chapter feasible in your situation?
5. What are the ages of your children/stepchildren? What special problems do you have with the different ages?

8

The Remarried Couple and Money

It was because of the subject of money that the coauthors, Dick and Carole, and Carole's husband-to-be, Henry, really got to know each other. This is how it happened.

When Henry and Carole reached the point at which they were anticipating marriage, they asked Dick to be the pastor at their wedding and he gladly agreed. In the early premarriage counseling sessions, their interest centered on the wedding. They wanted to build a meaningful wedding celebration that was an authentic description of themselves. And they found many ways to do it. They planned to use gifts of chalice, bread, wine, flowers, and a banner to be presented by various friends. They also planned to invite participation of Henry's young adult sons and Carole's younger children. A special friend and a brother-in-law would do readings. Further, they planned a Communion service; the first to be served would be the circle of their extended family. And they selected the music from among their favorite compositions and the instrumental musicians and vocalist from among their friends.

From time to time they discussed their relationship, their children, their joys and problems with each other. They appeared to have few problems and seemed to be dealing with those. They expressed a bouyant zest for living with each other and a love sparked with good humor. They really seemed to "have it all together."

Then, eight days before the wedding, Henry and Carole arrived at Dick's office to go over the final plans for the wedding. They were ashen and somber. They declared that they didn't know whether there would be a wedding or not. Henry had asked Carole to come to two appointments that afternoon. The earlier appointment was with an attorney, to discuss formulating a prenuptial agreement. Both Henry and Carole had not dealt with some of their fears and distrust about money, fears that surfaced in this session over making up the prenuptial agreement. Henry, though he loved Carole, was worried about his young adult sons. If he and Carole were later to divorce, he feared that his boys would not inherit what their father and their deceased mother had worked for many years to accumulate. So Henry wisely pushed the prenuptial agreement. Carole, on the other hand, had tried to avoid the issue of the prenuptial agreement. There had been many bitter fights in her first marriage over money. She was torn, feeling that Henry's boys should be adequately protected but at the same time feeling that she was not adequately protected. She saw Henry's concern as a stand for his sons and against her. So their discussion stalemated without conclusion.

At this impasse, they came to Dick's office. Though Dick had anticipated a light, happy planning session of a half hour or so, he fortunately had no other appointments. The three talked all afternoon. They explored the questions of what a man "owes" children of a previous marriage and what he "owes" a present wife. Three hours later, Henry and Carole had reached enough of an agreement (perhaps "truce" is the more accurate word) that they decided they would probably proceed with plans for the wedding.

For the entire week before the wedding they continued to argue about, discuss, and negotiate the prenuptial agreement. They drew both of their attorneys into it, seeking counsel and advice. On the morning of their wedding day, they again went to the attorney's office, still arguing about what was going to be in this document. Finally, they drew up an agreement. Since it was a Saturday and all secretaries had the day off, Carole typed it, and they both signed it—with reservations. Then they went on to their wedding rehearsal!

Carole and Henry's experience probably surprises no one intimately acquainted with remarriage. In Lucile Duberman's indepth study of eighty-

ㄴ ぐ ぢ ㄹ

eight remarried couples, she asked what they considered the major problem in their relationship. The problem mentioned at the top of the list—the one we discussed in the last chapter—was child rearing. Thirty-five percent of the husbands and 35 percent of the wives mentioned children as their major problem. The second-ranked problem was money. Twenty percent of the husbands and 16 percent of the wives listed money as *the* major problem in their relationship.[1] Many, many more would probably have mentioned money as *one* of the major problems with which they contend in their remarriage.

Money was a topic frequently discussed in our conversations with remarried persons. Often, these discussions about money sounded like unfinished business, sometimes with overtones of suspicion, distrust, or bitterness.

We are going to attempt to help you achieve some ease, comfort, success with each other in the area of money management. We will do so by raising five questions for discussion and examination.

What Resources Do We Bring to the Marriage?

What resources one has and brings to the remarriage is an underdiscussed matter. Lillian Messinger interviewed seventy remarried couples. From her interviews she got the following impressions:

The couples very often reported difficulties in the financial arrangements in the new household. Many of the remarried men admitted that they did not speak freely about their financial assets. Many remarried women also admitted to being rather secretive about what financial resources they brought into the marriage.

Some women confided that after experiencing one marital break up, they felt it necessary to keep some money aside because of the possibility of yet another divorce. Men seemed similarly uncertain about the new marriage and showed reluctance to revise wills, insurance, and property assets.

The study seemed to show that the financial area was a highly sensitive and poorly resolved one for many couples and seemed to be the visible expression of their hesitance to make a commitment to the new marriage.[2]

Such uneasiness, distrust, and fear in the area of finances does not make one optimistic about the marriages! Our counsel would be this: When you remarry, *at least give each other the gift of honesty.*

To be sure, there may be several legitimate ways of deciding what you do about your financial conditions. Probably the two of you will not absolutely agree on what way is best for you. You may have vigorous discussions, even arguments. But all this is healthier than an atmosphere of distrust. If you are so bruised that you are suspicious of all persons of the opposite sex in general, or of your potential marriage partner in particular, we suggest you postpone marriage until you are ready to trust. If you want to enter this marriage, do it with an atmosphere of honesty and trust that includes money matters.

To begin, each partner in the coming marriage will share information with each other about three matters.

What financial assets do I bring to this marriage? What do I have in savings, investments, and real estate? (How much investment have I accumulated in my housing? Should I sell it and pay off the debt and the realtor's fee?) What ongoing income from such sources as alimony/child support, stock dividends, or rents may I anticipate? If I am working, what is my average take-home pay? Tell your partner all the things you can think of. Allow him or her to raise all the questions he or she can think of.

What debts, financial responsibilities, and obligations do I have? What charges or outstanding obligations do I have yet to pay? If one person has rather large debts, he or she might want to share how this happened. Also worth discussing is "How I plan to work out of this." And if it is on the agenda, the information "I need your help on this" should also be shared.

Some of the present and future obligations will be obvious. A court order or agreement about child support can be clearly understood and anticipated.

But there is probably a more vague area of responsibility that should also be discussed. For example, one marriage partner may tell the other, "I feel an inner obligation to help my children get a good education, get launched into their careers, get started in their homes, which will go beyond any court order. Can you live with my choices to invest some caring and money in this direction?" Or perhaps one or both partners will need to say to the other, "My aging parents may need help and support from me, including financial help, one of these days. Are you willing to live with this possibility?" There may be other future responsibilities that the couple should discuss.

What possible plans, hopes, dreams, or fantasies do I have about the future that might affect our financial status?

—Am I hoping to go on to some sort of schooling? At what expense? Do I plan to stop working for a time to do it?

—Am I hoping to start my own business, perhaps involving a drastic reduction in income for a time?

—Am I hoping to withdraw from a well-paid but pressure-filled job to do something less time consuming at a reduction in income?

—Do my hopes and dreams mesh with those of my prospective partner? Do I support my partner's dreams and does he or she support mine? Or do these dreams threaten and upset? How serious are we about such possibilities?

Once the couple have made and discussed such financial self-disclosure, the next question is "What do we do about it?" If either or both have some financial resources, they seem to have three choices: (a) they can merge their assets and their obligations; (b) they can keep their assets and obligations separate; (c) they can figure out some combination of the two.

They can merge their assets and obligations. The wife of one couple with whom we visited had a home from a previous marriage, and the husband had no such assets. They sold the wife's home and bought a new one, more suitable to their merged family. The house, obtained with a down payment from the sale of the wife's house, was put in both names. She reasoned, "It was my money that made the purchase of the house possible. But my husband has worked harder and more consistently at earning income for our family. I work sometimes, but not as consistently as he, so I figure, it all comes out." This was a couple who seemed to have minimal difficulties in the area of financial management.

Another couple, a widow and a widower, described their decisions about money at the time they married:

"We decided that an inheritance from the husband's former in-laws should go just to his children. But beyond that we decided to will both our estates to our combined seven children. We stipulated that when one of us dies, the surviving spouse could live off the proceeds of the estate until his or her death. Our two salaries were treated as one income to be budgeted by both of us for the good of the whole family. We began to act as one family. All of our income is for both of us. This is meant as a statement of faith and intent for each other and for the kids. This is one of the best things we've done. It is positive; there are no ifs, ands, or buts. Our use of money is an affirmation that we're in this for good."

They can choose to keep their assets and obligations separate. This may sound untrusting, but we can think of reasons why this may be the appropriate way for some couples, at least for a while. These reasons could include the following:

—The wife is a financially aware and self-sufficient person who freely chooses to enter into this marriage relationship and who stays in it because she has committed to do so, not because she must do so for financial reasons.

—The wife needs to establish herself as an independent financial entity, with credit rating, credit cards, etc.

—Either partner needs—both for self and for the others involved—to be clear about what she or he has available to invest in other family members, including children of the former marriage and aging parents.

—Either partner needs financial resources to launch a business or obtain education and would prefer to do this independently.

They may choose some combination of the above, perhaps merging resources to obtain housing but keeping some other matters separate, at least for a time.

If there are large differences in the financial resources each partner brings to the marriage, how do the partners feel about this? Does the less prosperous partner feel powerless? obligated? unable to express opinions about financial matters? owned? How does the more prosperous partner feel? Such questions are worth discussing so that a couple may begin with as complete an understanding of each other as possible.

How Do We Manage the Ongoing Expenses of Living in Remarriage?

Once the remarried couple and family begin life together, they should give careful attention to the management of their family finances, for a number of reasons. Probably one or both had been single-parent families before they came together and had enjoyed the freedom of not having to discuss with anyone how money was to be spent. After remarriage, however, the couple need to plan their finances carefully. One reason for this is that they do not know the exact expenses and needs of their new family unit. Another is that no two persons have the same priorities with regard to spending money. If either or both spend money only according to their own priorities, personal resentment and unnecessary financial pressures may result. Then, too, it is possible—even probable—that money was one of the points of contention in either or both of the terminated marriages, and so learning new ways of settling money differences is important to help the new couple avoid repeating those hassles; one or both partners may have endured financial difficulties brought about by previous spending patterns. Counselors have noted a close tie between able economic management and family stability.[3]

For any or all of the above reasons, it is important for the couple to make plans together and to begin a new, mutually agreed upon style of financial management, with new decisions, new habits, and new methods.

Values influence economic behavior, and so the way to begin developing a style of financial management is by asking the value questions about one's family life. "What are the goals and purposes of this family? What do we want to happen for the family collectively and for each of its members? What resources do we possess, and how can we better utilize them toward the realization of our objectives?"[4] Discussion on such matters may help the family to make decisions about priorities when there is not enough money for everything.

Before talking about the financial plan itself, consider three preliminary notes on budgeting from Sylvia Porter.[5]

1. Work together, making your plan a joint project. Talk about a wide variety of issues before trying to put down a single budget figure. The system that almost always feeds conflict is the one in which there is an arbitrary "boss" who imposes his or her plan on the family without discussion.[6]

2. Provide for personal allowances for each partner. One couple felt an increase of freedom when they budgeted a twenty-five-dollar monthly allowance for each partner. Wives should *not* be asked for an itemized account of what happened to food money. Budgets should *not* become straight jackets.

3. Keep records simple. Provide a plan for each month's spending, a history of where the money goes, and an overall picture to help you make decisions when a financial emergency arises.

Porter suggests four basic forms to use in creating a personal money-management system. Form I is a record of family income. Write down *all* the income the family can reasonably expect in any month, using the form included here or a similar one. Be accurate and realistic.

Porter points out that the family must anticipate three types of outgoing funds: (1) unavoidable expenses for big items such as insurance, mortgage, personal debts, taxes, etc.; these items must be paid no matter how inconvenient; (2) savings and emergency reserves; and (3) living expenses for every day.[7]

Form I Family Income[8]

WHAT WE WILL GET FROM	JAN.	FEB.	MAR.	APR.	MAY	JUNE	JULY	AUG.	SEPT.	OCT.	NOV.	DEC.	YEARLY TOTAL	NOTES
Husband's job														
Wife's job														
Business interests														
Interest														
Dividends														
Rent														
Gifts														
Company bonus or bonuses														
Tax refunds														
Moonlighting or jobs														
Profits from sales														
Alimony														
?														
?														
?														
Totals for the month														

She suggests that you record items one and two—unavoidable expense and necessary savings—on a second form, similar to Form II. Some will want to add committed giving to church and charities on this list as well, possibly putting it at the top of the list.

Porter's Form III can help you to discover what the family has available for day-to-day expenses.

Decisions on how to distribute money for day-to-day expenses can be shown on Form IV.

Incidentally, when creating a record system, any parent receiving child-support payments should keep records of the actual amount expended on each child as a basis for any discussions that might arise.

If both partners have incomes, the remarried couple must make a decision on how the incomes are to be distributed. They can merge their incomes, budgeting together essentially as outlined in the preceding section, giving themselves adequate allowances to cover personal spending and the amount needed to carry on their work (meal money, travel money, clothing money, and so on). Or they can keep their own incomes and each contribute 50

Form II Fixed Expenses - Including Savings[9]

WHAT WE MUST SPEND AND SAVE	JAN.	FEB.	MAR.	APR.	MAY	JUNE	JULY	AUG.	SEPT.	OCT.	NOV.	DEC.	YEAR'S TOTAL	NOTES
Rent or mortgage														
Fuel bills														
Telephone														
Electricity, gas														
Water														
Installment payment A														
Installment payment B														
Education (or other) payment														
Real estate taxes														
Income taxes														
Home and life insurance														
Auto insurance														
Medical, dental														
What we must set aside for savings alone														
Other														
Totals for each Month														

Form III Day-to-Day Expenses[10]

	JAN.	FEB.	MAR.	APR.	MAY	JUNE	JULY	AUG.	SEPT.	OCT.	NOV.	DEC.
From Form I, your monthly income	$											
From Form II, the total of your unavoidable expenses and savings for the year, divided by 12.	$											
What you have available for your day-to-day living expenses	$											

percent of the money needed to cover family expenses and savings, forming individual spending, saving, or investing plans for the rest. However, one wife in a couple who did this felt the system was unfair. Because she earned less than her husband, half of the household took proportionately more of her income than of her husband's.

Form IV Budgeting Day-to-Day Expenses[11]

WHAT WE WILL SPEND FOR DAY-TO-DAY LIVING THIS MONTH	JAN.	FEB.	MAR.	APR.	MAY	JUNE	JULY	AUG.	SEPT.	OCT.	NOV.	DEC.	NOTES
For food and related items	$	$	$	$	$	$	$	$	$	$	$	$	
For household services and expenses													
For furnishings and equipment													
For clothes													
For transportation													
For medical care													
For personal care													
For education and recreation													
For gifts and contributions													
For other things and non-things													
TOTAL													
Total available for the month (from last line of form III)	$	$	$	$	$	$	$	$	$	$	$	$	

An alternate plan would be for the couple to keep their own incomes and each contribute an appropriate percentage of the total household expenses. For example, one partner would contribute 60 percent (if that partner's income were 60 percent of the total income) and the other partner's 40 percent. Another couple might choose to keep their own incomes and each contribute for certain expenses. As an example, Sylvia Porter suggests that the husband might take over payment of bills such as rent, mortgage, insurance, taxes, or the like. The wife might take over payment of home-management bills—food, entertainment at home, ordinary household overhead. She suggests extra entertainment at home or extra household help might be the wife's expense, while entertainment "out" might be the husband's.[12]

Porter points out that these are just examples and suggests that every couple work out their own plan, so long as they discuss ideas freely and do not harbor any secret resentments. The best plan is the one that is chosen after an open discussion between the two partners, even if it represents a compromise for both. Our impression is that couples who both contribute some income seem to have an easier time making financial decisions. Having income does give a partner some influence and power when a couple is making financial decisions, like it or not.

For couples in which one partner is not generating income outside the home, the decisions may be more difficult. One wife and mother of three told us, "I'm in a double bind. Even though we (she and her children) bring a lot to my present husband, we take a lot, too. Even though intellectually I can say, 'He knew what he was getting into,' I wind up feeling guilty because I have kids and they do cost money. That is not healthy. One of my kids will tell me they need a particular pair of shoes for a choir performance and I ask myself, 'Where am I going to get the money?' At times I sneak around on purchases like that, and I shouldn't do that. I don't like feeling guilty, angry, or ashamed because I have kids and my kids have needs. But that's the way it is some days.''

If one marriage partner is not employed outside the home, both need to recognize and value the contribution the person makes in household management, food preparation, child care, chauffering, and all the rest, so that both feel the person at home has the right to equal involvement in decision making about finances.

One other matter in family money management is the subject of allowances for children. Particularly if children from two previous households come together in the new stepfamily, it will be important to establish new ground rules and fair treatment for all, in the area of allowances. Sylvia Porter offers counsel on allowances. Give children allowances as soon as they can understand the use of money for buying things they want. Give an allowance to young children to cover a very short period of time and just a few items. Then expand the time and the number of items that it covers. There should be a clear understanding between parents and child on what the allowance is to cover, so that the child does not "put the bite" on the uninformed parent for items he or she should be buying with his or her allowance. Allowances should be renegotiated at least once a year. The child should have full responsibility for spending his or her own allowance. If mistakes are made with allowances, the child should accept responsibility and put up with the results. As the child gets older, he or she should be given increasing responsibility for budgeting an allowance, learning to manage bank accounts, and learning to use credit. Then the young adult child will be ready to take financial responsiblity for his or her own life. [13]

How Do We Deal with Future Financial Decisions?

The person who has done everything possible to provide for those he or she loves will want to do the best possible for those same persons after he or she dies. A person's will may be the most important document he or she signs in a lifetime. [14] A will is essential in order to:

—provide for one's loved ones in the best possible way;
—dispose of one's belongings in the manner one chooses;
—avoid conflict over one's intentions after one has died;
—reveal aspects of one's financial affairs that may not be known to others so that final details can be taken care of;
—facilitate the care of one's minor children;
—save many expenses.

Many of the misunderstandings that keep one from making out a will are simply not true. In writing a will, one does not need to make an itemized list of assets and dispose of them one by one. A person may change his or her will as often as he or she wishes. The existence of a will in no way inhibits a person's ability to sell or otherwise dispose of property. A person can act as if he or she had not written a will. One need not put one's business into good shape before making out a will. [15]

One does need, however, a fairly clear idea of how one wants to dispose of one's assets at death. A competent attorney can then draw up the rest of the will with a minimum of time and expense.

While making a will is not a difficult step to take for something so worthwhile, it is one many remarried people avoid. One reason for avoidance is generally shared: people simply do not like to think of their own death. But making a will is avoided by remarried people for yet another reason. A will is "a barometer of feelings." [16] When you write your will you must answer these difficult questions: "How, after my death, do I say to my children, my spouse, my stepchildren, perhaps my former spouse, what I want to say through the disposal of my estate? What is it that I want to say? How do I say it with wisdom, justice, and fairness?"

Persons may overcomplicate this question. If one were to die suddenly while one still had minor children, one would certainly want his or her assets used to raise the children to independent adulthood and to provide resources to help one's spouse make the transition to some other life-style.

Perhaps a person would want to give money to causes one believed in; at least one would want to fulfill one's last year's pledge to the church. Beyond that, well, let's face it. How many people have resources beyond that?

It is not morbid to ask, "If I were to die today, how would I want my resources distributed?" and then to have a will drawn that expresses the answer.

How Do We Deal with "More-than-Money" Issues?

Objection: We're making this too simple. When we talk about money, we talk about more than money!

So far, we have been oversimplifying money questions. We have been discussing them as if the subject of money were an objective, rational topic. If that were so, life would be simple! While it is important to look at finances objectively, it is equally important to recognize the many feelings we have about the subject of money.

For one thing, there is the emotional impact of our *cultural* experience with money. Our culture is one that seems to place great value on money. If we ask persons in our culture what money means, we will probably get a variety of answers. Money means power, status, security, pleasure, and happiness.

While it is ridiculous to ignore the fact that money is an important commodity in our culture, it is also foolish to overemphasize its importance. Perhaps one should stop at times and ask, "After my basic needs have been met, what of the things I most want in life can be provided by money?" Perhaps we are ready to hear Jesus' words: ". . . A person's real life in no way depends upon the number of his or her possessions" (Luke 12:15b, author's paraphrase). Perhaps we are also ready to hear the words of modern prophets that America's standard of living has peaked and that our earth's frail ecosystem can no longer support the extravagant, wasteful life-style we live.

On the next emotional level is the *family* experience of money. In the remarried family, money is often a highly emotional issue. The emotion surrounding money issues most often touches stepfathers and confronts them with a "money riddle." A remarried man often finds himself contributing to the support of two households and having both women suspect that he's not doing well by them. His current wife may resent what he pays to his former family, and his former wife may resent equally what he gives to his present family. He may in turn suspect that both wives are using money as a weapon to test loyalties and love. He may begin to look at the persons in both of his families as vultures.[17]

One mother vividly illustrated this kind of conflict. She recalled, "My daughter started clarinet lessons. We called my former husband and asked him to pay a month's rent on the clarinet, sixteen bucks. He said he couldn't afford it, and he didn't pay it. Soon after, he bought a new organ for his present wife. The kids are really angry about that. It will be a long time before they forgive him. It's a bad situation and it's not going to get any better until the kids are raised and no money changes hands."

Other family members sense the money conflict as well. A grown stepdaughter comments, "I think the subject of money is interesting because it is symbolic on the one hand, and it ain't symbolic on the other hand. I've always been curious to know how much my stepbrother and stepsister have been financially supported and helped through college by Dad and Christy (her stepmother) so that I can compare how much I've been helped."[18]

A first wife comments, "I guess if I'm really honest with myself, I have to chuckle to myself when I realize I'm causing them [her former husband and his wife] a lot of problems in their marriage [by asking for increased child support]. That's a very nasty thing to say, and not very mature. But I still have to admit that it kind of makes me feel good."

In all the literature we read about remarriage, practically all comments about money centered on the highly emotional conflict that occurs in stepfamilies over the subject of money. Observers of remarriage bemoan the fact that there is no standard, legislated agreement about what support a father in a certain income bracket should give in support of his children. The court judgments vary tremendously. The vagueness about what a man should do for his children tends to make this a conflict-prone subject. It seems that everyone says to the father-stepfather, "Father, give me my share of the property" (Luke 15:12, NEB). But when the father-stepfather adds up what people feel is their share, it comes to somewhere between 150 percent and 300 percent of what he actually has. In turn, he feels stressed, strained, and angry.

Is there an escape from this family money trap? The father-stepfather can look within and ask himself if he is perhaps overpaying out of guilt, remorse, or eagerness to escape conflict. If so, perhaps he can make more realistic decisions as to how he will respond to money requests. We offer other suggestions in the next section.

Money is also a highly emotional matter on the *individual level* at times. The individual may be looking to money to do things that it cannot do; it cannot provide the esteem or satisfaction that is lacking elsewhere in life. For example, Paul Schurman tells of counseling a man who was deeply in debt, not from buying necessities but from spending money on expensive hobbies he could not afford. As they probed into what was going on in this man's life, it became clear that "Fred was attempting to compensate for his failure to work out meaningful relationships in personal and professional life by buying himself expensive presents."[19] For that reason, Schurman urges us to look deeper when we have money problems. He suggests that a couple ask themselves, "Is the problem one that financial counseling will help us to solve (when factual, logical budgeting plans will suffice), or is our money problem a symptom of some deeper problem?" He notes that financial institutions say that 80 percent of the families they help out of financial difficulty are back in financial trouble within two years.[20]

Money has significance on cultural, family, and personal levels. It stirs strong emotions within us.

What Can We Do to Increase Harmony in the Financial Area of Our Remarried Family Life?

As long as people use money, there will be some tensions among those who have to make financial decisions. Some steps can be taken, however, to reduce such tensions to livable dimensions. Some of those steps are the following:

1. The couple partners can tell each other their financial attitude history. Each can share such information as this: "When I was a child the attitude toward money in our family was . . . . The availability of money in our family was . . . . In my life, I felt richest when . . . . I felt poorest when . . . . Two or three people that most strongly influenced my attitude about money were . . . . Two or three events that most strongly influenced my attitude about money were . . . ." One at a time the partners can listen and raise questions till each understands the history that contributes to the spouse's present attitudes and behaviors with money.

2. As mentioned earlier, the couple can be honest with each other about the financial resources and obligations each brings to the marriage. Such

reservations are rarely a secret to the partner any way. We believe that for some couples prenuptial agreements can be helpful in protecting the rights of both parties. Such agreements should be worked through in an atmosphere of openness and trust long before the wedding is to take place. This process may clarify plans and provide a secure feeling for all parties.

3. The partners in the marriage can attempt to be consistent, maintaining the same financial point of view *after* the wedding as they had *before* it. In our interviews, we sometimes heard complaints like these:

SHE: "He changed, particularly in the area of money, after we got married. Before, when we were dating, we didn't always spend a lot of money, but if we did, he didn't seem to care. He came across as a very generous person, very relaxed about money. Now he raises a fuss about the tiniest spending for fun. He gripes a lot about the regular bills, too. I discover I just didn't know who he was in regard to money."

HE: "When we were dating, she was very considerate of me and what I had to spend. And I had a little more then, which I enjoyed spending on her. But I didn't realize—and she didn't tell me—what huge obligations I'd be taking on when I married her and began helping to support her kids. Dating and marriage are two different things; I wish she could understand that she has larger expectations than I can meet."

Don't hide from each other. Try to be the same persons with each other before and after the wedding.

4. The couple can explore each other's values in regard to money. Here is a way—a "fun," nonthreatening way—to talk abut values and attitudes in regard to money. Read over the following set of statements about money. Put a check mark [√] by three or four that most accurately describe your feelings. (Or add other statements and put your check mark by those.) Put an X by the three or four statements that seem to you to represent your partner's values most accurately.

Here's the list:

a. Save for a rainy day.
b. I can't take it with me.
c. Money is a convenience. I love it, not for what it is, but for the things I can do with it.
d. Money represents security. I like to save it so I know I can meet future obligations and crises.
e. Why spend it?

f. Why not spend it?

g. Enjoy! Life's too short!!

h. When I'm down in the dumps, I go buy something. It really picks me up.

i. When I buy something I don't need, I really feel awful. I ask myself over and over again why I spent that money.

j. I just love giving gifts, to family, to friends, to church. I enjoy money in great measure to have something to give.

k. Don't dip into the capital.

l. I only go around once in life, so I should live it with all the gusto I can.

m. Money isn't very important to me.

n. Money is very important to me.

o. The best things in life are free.

p. The best things in life are free, but somebody has to pay the rent.

q. Be careful with money; there may be a depression around the corner.

r. On the other hand, the depression may never come, and I would have worried for nothing.

After you have checked this list for what is closest to how you feel and how you think your partner feels, then share that information with each other and discuss it. Don't accuse or put down. (None of the statements are intended to be negative. However, a person's feelings may make some of them seem so.) Both partners should share what statements they picked, tell why, and tell about experiences that popped into their minds as they picked the item.

Perhaps the individuals would like to take the statements they checked about themselves and combine them into a short paragraph on the subject "What Money Seems to Mean to Me." Whether or not they do that, the couple should go on to discuss with each other, "Where are we similar to each other in our attitudes to money, and where are we different?"

In all of this procedure, we urge that neither partner try to change the other, simply try to understand him or her.

5. Persons can recognize that money problems arise basically because after remarriage they have less money to go more places. As Jessie Bernard noted, "As compared to first marriages, second marriages are decidedly handicapped so far as income is concerned."[21]

There will be legitimate differences of opinion as to the financial rights and responsibilities of former spouses. It is regrettable that more consistent rules and norms do not exist. However, the recognition that any solution will be a compromise and that everyone will want or need more than is available, is an important milestone. Once this insight is achieved, perhaps former spouses can discuss money as a single issue. This kind of negotiation can minimize old angers, jealousies, and competitions and keep children from becoming pawns in the power play between spouses. Some vigorous confrontations may have to occur before discussions of money between ex-spouses can be reasonably logical, but such a goal is desirable for the happiness and welfare of all persons involved.

6. The individuals in the couple can allow each other to have differences in regard to money.

Jackie and Jeff Herrigan, in their book *Loving Free*, tell how they achieved this goal of accepting each other. They had had their share of money hassles. Indeed, money was a frequent source of friction for them. Finally, they discovered their primary issue. They discovered that each time money had become a problem, it was because one of them hadn't understood why the money was being spent. Each of their arguments boiled down to either a lack of shared goals or a lack of com-munication.[22]

They decided that before they had any more arguments they should look at their spending and try to make their use of money a positive force in their marriage. When they examined the different areas in their budget, they were surprised to discover that the areas straining the budget weren't the utility bills, groceries, or mortgage, for these bills remained fairly constant. "Our budget problems usually were telephone (Jeff), arts and crafts supplies (me), cosmetics, beauty shop, etc. (me), gambling (Jeff); records (me), and books (both of us)."[23]

The pattern suddenly became clear. In each area of overspending one partner was fulfilling a need. Jackie went on to explain how each of those items holds great importance for one of them. She said they discovered that the problem wasn't the amount of money or even how it was spent. It was, rather, that they had not explained to each other why they frequently overspent on the same things. Once that became clear, both were willing to let the other use any available money to fulfill those needs, to relax, to grow.

They decided that their philosophy of money was based on the hope that money would be a life-giving force in their marriage. They felt that money should help people feel more free, not enslaved. They chose the course that whatever money remained after basic bills were covered should be spent to bring happiness to each of them as individuals, to both of them as couple, and to others.[24]

And so, they changed their system of bookkeeping once more. They stopped the joint checking accounts and opened separate accounts. Each partner had certain responsibilities to cover, but once those were dealt with, the money that remained was considered play money for which they did not have to answer to the other partner or anyone else. She concludes, "The atmosphere had changed. No more allowances, no more my money, your money divisions. Only our money, with spending limited by the sole question 'Is it meaningful spending to one of us?'"[25]

7. Persons can live their lives in the larger stewardship context. Jesus very clearly taught us that we are managers of all with which we are entrusted. The Greek term *oikonomos* meant "manager of a household." This is the term from which our words "economics" and "economist" come. We are temporary managers, economists, of life and resources, and we are accountable for our use of all with which we are entrusted. That's not a bad perspective to remember when real or imagined financial injustices happen to us, when hard decisions about the use of scarce funds have to be faced.

Perhaps this vision of ourselves as trusted managers of God's resources is the broad and ultimate vision we need in order to reduce our money problems to manageable size.

Questions for Reflection

1. What unforeseen problems concerning money have surfaced in your remarriage?
2. Have you been truthful with your remarriage partner concerning money? If not, why?
3. Given the facts of your combined financial situation, how are you going to handle the finances? How do both partners *feel* about this new system?
4. What are the goals and purposes of this family? What do you want for the family collectively and for each of its members?
5. If you are a two-paycheck family, how is your money handled? Do you both consider the present system fair?
6. Have you written your wills? What kinds of problems could surface when you consider how you and your spouse want your estates divided?

Creative Conflict in Remarriage

It is a strange experience, first to read what the experts say about conflict management in marriage and then to listen to remarried people talk about the same subject. The first group is positive about conflict; the second group is negative about conflict. The first group values conflict for the creative potential inherent in an effective conflict-resolution process; the latter group fears conflict because of the possibility that it might destroy everything they hold dear.

We trust that there is important wisdom in what both groups say. So we shall report first what we heard from one and then what we learned from the other. Then we will try to discover, in the light of all this, how the remarried couple can engage in creative conflict.

The Voice of the Experts

"A fight a day keeps the marriage counselor away," said one psychiatrist.[1]

John Scanzoni adds, "Conflict per se is not a sign of ill health. Quite the contrary! It can be a sure indication of health, vigor, and vitality!"[2]

David Augsburger enthusiastically agrees, "Conflict is natural, normal, neutral, and sometimes even delightful. . . . Conflict is neither good nor bad, right nor wrong. Conflict simply is."[3]

Not only do these specialists affirm the importance of conflict; they also point to the danger of its absence. Writes David Johnson, "A conflict-free relationship may be only a sign that you have no relationship at all, not that you have a good relationship."[4]

Sylvia Ashton-Warner agrees as she shares a memory:

> A woman said to me once so proudly, "My family *never* quarrels." I was young at the time and our children were young and I thought, "How wonderful! If only I could say that." But I'm not young now and I know better. When I look back on that family who never quarreled I remember their passivity; the slow eyes that did not flash; on the parents' faces, no grooves that tears had scoured. I know now that it takes passion and energy to make a quarrel . . . of the magnificent sort . . . magnificent reconciliations; the surging and soaring of magnificent feeling.[5]

Other testimony could be added. These gifted marriage professionals agree on this point: conflict is natural and normal; conflict can be zestful and delightful; conflict helps a couple deal with matters that will lead them to deeper intimacy. Oh to be sure, conflict can be misused and abused so that it has sadder consequences. But the best course for a couple is to recognize and express their conflict (not deny and suppress it) and find ways that they can create "win-win" situations out of their conflict.

The Voice of Remarried Persons

When we turn from these outstanding authorities on married life to remarried persons themselves, we hear quite a different view on conflict in marriage. Many remarried persons feel that in their first marriages they either engaged in conflict in all the wrong ways, or were the victim of someone who did, or both. They have vivid memories of "lose-lose" conflicts in their previous marriages, and they have a good deal of uncertainty about conflict in the present marriage. This is for many reasons.

One person told us, "Whenever I get in a fight with my present spouse, it's as though a voice whispers in my ear, 'You failed last time, and you're going to fail again!'"

Others resist conflict because they fear that they have fallen into all the bad habits of conflict about which the counselors warn. One type of conflict that counselors urge a couple to avoid is the "round robin" or "merry-go-round'' fight, the argument that goes round and round and never is resolved. But as one remarried man told us, ''When I find myself arguing with my second wife about the same things I argued with my first wife about, and when I hear myself saying the same things I said then and hear my present wife saying almost the same things my former wife said, I know I'm doing something wrong.''

Still others told us, ''I don't feel in a strong enough position in our relationship to raise any problems. I know we'd both feel better if we got some of these things settled. But frankly, I'm afraid to start for fear I will rock the boat so much that he or she will leave me.''

And yet other partners mention that they subdue arguments between themselves because these confrontations are so frightening to children who were traumatized by fights in an earlier marriage. One stepfather, noting how upset the children were because of a couple fight, asked the little boy, ''Why does it make you so upset when your mother and I fight? You and your sisters fight all the time.'' ''But we can't divorce each other,'' the little boy replied.

Fear of failure, bad memories of ''merry-go-round'' fights or ''Mt. Vesuvius'' fights, uncertainty about the strength of the present marriage, concern that the children will be upset—all these factors and more inhibit remarried persons from entering into wholehearted conflict with each other, even if it would be helpful for them to do so.

However, some remarried persons are discovering that conflict is necessary and are gingerly finding their way into it, sometimes successfully, sometimes not. We asked the remarried couples that we interviewed how they handled conflict. These are some of their answers which, they readily admit include some healthy and some unhealthy responses.

''We bring a lot of bad habits from our previous marriages. He tries to kid me out of what I want or otherwise avoids my confrontation. This infuriates me all the more. But if I keep at it, eventually he hears me, at least a little.''

''I give her the silent treatment. She gives me the screaming treatment.''

HE: ''She gunnysacks. She clams up about what is bothering her, and months later, she bites my head off about it.''
SHE: ''He wants me to talk, but I know that I will say things that hurt, so I clam up.''

"I really work at handling conflict constructively in this marriage. Anyone would be a damn fool to go through a divorce again."

"I have learned that some things aren't as important as I thought in my first marriage. I am sad to see some of my divorced friends avoiding remarriage for fear of conflict. In spite of conflicts, life is so much more enjoyable when shared."

SHE: "Silence, initially, then bargaining."
HE: "Anger, silence, then explosion; then I apologize and retreat, usually."
BOTH: "Eventually we negotiate and then really make up."

These couples are discovering that second marriages can survive conflict. Sometimes they are even strengthened by it. None of them would pretend that they know all the answers about creative conflict in second marriages. Nor do we. But let us capitalize on what these remarried persons and the marriage experts have to tell us and see what we can discover in response to this next subject.

Managing Conflict

How then should remarried persons manage conflict in their relationship? We offer some suggestions for successful conflict management, with special reference to remarriage. While some of these suggestions imply a progression through an argument, they are not really eleven separate steps but are components that operate in the lives of those who resolve conflict successfully.

First, build individual self-esteem, both in yourself and in your partner. Conflict is not overwhelmingly threatening to healthy, happy persons who feel good about themselves and who have a sense of their own personal power.

We talked with people who do not initiate a needed conflict because they feel their partner is in such a bad spot, feeling so negative or unsure, that one more confrontation would just destroy that person. This is too bad, for many reasons. Postponing needed conflict settlement is not going to strengthen the relationship. However, one needs to be sensitive to the readiness or willingness of the partner to deal with conflict or criticism. A sensitive person will not hit her or his partner in the "bread basket" unless the emotional "muscles" are firm and ready for the blow.

Building and affirming strength in yourself and in your partner should be a high priority. Affirming what you treasure, complimenting what you like, celebrating the victories of your partner are ways to begin building the personal strength that can handle conflict successfully. (Such support should flow both ways between partners, but a person should learn to give such affirmation and recognition to oneself as well.)

Second, affirm and strengthen your relationship with each other. In particular, make clear that this is a long-term, permanent commitment. Conflict will not end this relationship but may, in fact, strengthen it.

One remarried wife told us, "Intimacy is contaminated by fear of abandonment. I know whenever my husband, Jake, is disgusted with me, I find myself trying to rationalize how I can get along without him. Fear of being abandoned is still in the back of my head."

So we would counsel remarried partners to tell their mates how much they enjoy, relish, value, and cherish their marriage, and how much they are committed to making it work. We would urge persons to give their spouses such messages when there is no conflict, when a conflict is beginning, when a conflict is in progress, and when a conflict has ended. We would urge against any verbal or nonverbal threats to leave the marriage or to put the other partner out.

We would encourage remarried partners to try very hard to see conflict as normal and inevitable, urging them to do their arguing with acceptance and trust. "Acceptance is the unconditional affirmation of the other as other, without taking a judgmental or accusatory stance toward him/her . . . . Acceptance begets acceptance and estrangement begets estrangement. Trust is also catching."[6]

Third, when you sense a conflict, ask yourself, "Is this our (my present spouse's and my) battle?" Psychologists have long noted the problem of *displaced* anger, which occurs when a person directs the anger that he or she feels toward a certain person or situation toward someone else. Some remarried persons in conflict tell us that this is a particularly acute issue for them. Smouldering resentments toward a former spouse, seemingly forgotten hurts inflicted by that spouse, and unresolved conflicts with that former spouse all invade and contaminate the present relationship. So sometimes when a person is doing battle with a present marriage partner, he or she is really fighting the former one! The present marriage partner may be bewildered and troubled by such a conflict.

Of course, other influences invade the couple's relationship also. Work conditions; conflicts with colleagues, customers, or bosses; emotional cycles and mood swings in both men and women—all these can be part of a conflict as well.

We are not saying that a person should be silent about any of these unresolved matters with former spouse or with others outside the relationship. Perhaps they need to be discussed with an able pastor or marriage counselor. We are not saying, either, that you should overanalyze a potential conflict with your mate. Probably no one ever launders out all the extraneous influences in any conflict. Yet it is reasonable for partners to ask themselves, "Do I have a legitimate beef here, or is something else bugging me so that I'm trying to pick a fight? In other words, is this my problem (my need to deal with my own feelings and history) or the relationship's problem (something that exists primarily between my wife or husband and me)?"

If it is your problem, you still may want to talk it over with your spouse, but in a different way, such as "I need to talk with you about something that's troubling me. You didn't particularly contribute to it, but now you're a part of it in some way. Here's how it is. . . ." If the conflict is with your spouse, approach it a different way; more on that in a moment.

Fourth, admit, accept, and take responsibility for your own anger. That's hard to do. Practice saying out loud, "I am angry." Somehow, large parts of our society have made it a virtue never to be angry, or more accurately, to deny anger. But anger is there, and it is real. What is anger? David Augsburger helps us understand anger by reconstructing what frequently happens in most human relationships:

> (1) I feel keen frustration in my relationship with another; (2) I see the other person as rejecting me—my worth, my needs, my freedom, my request; (3) I become suddenly and intensely anxious; (4) I blow away my anxiety with anger which confuses things even further; (5) I may then feel guilty for my behavior and resentful of the other's part in the painful experience.[7]

This guilt seemingly comes because many Christians believe that Jesus taught that we should never be angry. They think particularly of Jesus' statement in Matthew 5, when Jesus says that though the old law is not to murder, in his new kingdom "everyone who is angry with his brother shall be liable to judgment . . ." (Matthew 5:22a, RSV). They absolutize this verse and ignore Jesus' own behavior when he expressed anger freely on occasion. Further, some Bible scholars have noted that the New English Bible translates this most accurately: "Anyone who nurses anger against his brother must be brought to the judgment'' (Matthew 5:22a, NEB). There is quite a difference between the two translations; if the NEB view is right, Jesus is not forbidding anger itself. Anger just *is* and comes inevitably in times of anxiety. Rather, Jesus is urging us not to ''nurse'' our anger; that is, not to keep suppressing it and letting it build up but, instead, to deal with it. Jesus' teaching seems to lead in the opposite direction from what many people think. It leads in the direction of healthily resolving anger rather than denying or suppressing it. As the writer of Ephesians puts it, ''Be angry but do not sin; do not let the sun go down on your anger'' (Ephesians 4:26, RSV). Anger should be kept current, dealt with day by day, and not allowed to accumulate.

It's OK to be angry. Without anger there would be no conflict and no making up. You need to admit your anger, accept it, and take responsibility for it. You need to be able to say out loud, ''I am angry.''

Fifth, confront the person with whom you are angry. To be sure, it is hard to confront. Most persons (and remarried persons especially) have memories of painful fights that went nowhere, that only hurt the participants. They think, ''Is this going to be another one? Maybe I'd better avoid it, postpone it, ignore it; maybe the problem will go away on its own.'' That fear of confronting is understandable. Although you should be sensitive about the appropriateness of the times you choose for confronting, you should not avoid necessary confrontation. To confront is to choose, deliberately, to help you both to examine the consequences of your behavior. To confront is to invite self-examination.[8]

Howard Clinebell, well-known pastoral counselor, suggests, ''Confrontation plus caring brings growth just as judgment plus grace brings salvation.''[9] At least, caring plus confrontation brings a person an opportunity to change and grow.

Confrontations should be accompanied by words and acts of love. David Augsburger calls this combination ''care-fronting.'' It is a combination statement that includes elements of both columns that follow:

Caring	*Confronting*
I care about our relationship.	I feel deeply about the issue at stake.
I want to hear your view.	I want to clearly express mine.
I want to respect your insights.	I want respect for mine.
I trust you to be able to handle my honest feelings.	I want you to trust me with yours.

I promise to stay with the discussion until we've reached an understanding.	I want you to keep working with me until we've reached a new understanding.
I will not trick, pressure, manipulate, or distort the differences.	I want your unpressured, clear, honest view of our differences.
I give you my loving, honest respect.	I want your caring-confronting response.[10]

And so, difficult though confrontation may be, it is important for you to confront your partner when a behavior or situation is troubling you.

Sixth, adopt some mutually agreed upon styles, methods, and rules for "fair fighting." This is difficult to do because people have inherited and developed many different ways of handling conflict.

—Some eagerly seek it, and others rigorously avoid it.

—Some love it and some hate it.

—Some enjoy expressing a full range of emotions, and some are careful to control their emotions during an argument.

—Some like to "let it fly." They attack, call names, and so forth, and then promptly forget all that was said during the argument. Others remember every jibe or name for years afterwards.

—Some like to argue primarily through words, while others use mostly symbols, actions, objects (such as gifts) to signal the beginning and end of conflict.

—A few have joyful memories connected with conflict while most have painful memories.

—Some persons withhold affection and sexual activity during a conflict until it is somehow resolved; others seek affection and sexual activity in the midst of the period of conflict as an expression that the couple is still together.

It is likely that any couple will have to unlearn some conflict habits, learn some new skills, and develop a new style of conflict with which they both can live. Sometime, when there is no active conflict between the marriage partners, they should talk about and agree upon a mutual style and the ground rules for their conflicts with each other.

Here are some ground rules that some couples have included: (You should make a list that fits your relationship. Your list will include only what you select from the following list, plus other specific guidance that is right for you.)

1. Have arguments by appointment. George Bach suggests that a couple

"warm up" by what he calls "deutero-fighting," which is conflict over *when* to have the face-to-face discussion, *where* to have it, and *what* the precise topic will be. Then both come to it ready and reasonably willing. No one is subject to a surprise attack.[11]

2. Do not use physical violence.

3. Drink no alcohol, or a minimum of alcohol, before the scheduled conflict.

4. Don't hit below the belt (a person's areas of personal vulnerability).

5. Don't wear your belt around your neck (don't be overly defensive).

6. As much as possible, have conflicts over specific, mutually agreed upon issues.

7. As much as possible, have conflicts over current issues. Try to leave the past out of this discussion.

8. Try hard to understand what each is saying. Ask for clarification. Give feedback to each other to be sure you are understanding each other. There is healing in knowing that one is heard and understood, even if the issue of the conflict remains. Don't assume that you know what your partner is thinking. Always check it out, even if it seems obvious.

9. Don't try to find solutions too soon. Be sure that you both understand the issue and that you express and perceive the depth of emotion surrounding it.

10. Don't be sarcastic with each other.

11. Allow either partner to call for a time out, which may last five minutes, an hour, or days. One or both of you may need time to cool off, to meditate, or to think about what the other has said. However, you should agree upon a time when the conflict will be resumed.[12]

Seventh, explore the issues and your feelings about the issues, using, as best you can, the rules for fair arguments that you have chosen. Of course, there will be variations in the conflicts, depending on how large the issue and how strongly either or both of you feel about it.

If one partner has a grievance that has long been buried (perhaps not even recognized for a long time by that person herself or himself), then perhaps that person needs to be an erupting "Vesuvius" for a while. Probably the receiving partner will do best to listen, to ask questions, and to clarify. The partner may be wise not to defend for a while, even if at the outset the statements seem extreme and unfair. Try to understand the issue, how the person is feeling, and why he or she feels it so strongly.

This ventilating of the issue will proceed much more clearly if the person expressing the grievance can master the skill advocated by many persons in the field of communication, the skill of using "I" messages rather than "you" messages. In this type of communication the person talks about oneself, what "I" am experiencing, what "I" am feeling, what "I" am needing. The person does not say what "you" are doing, or that "you" are making the person feel bad, or that "you" don't care about his or her needs. "I" messages can usually be heard without a sense of attack. "You" messages often put the receiver on the defensive.

Perhaps this is a way in which remarried people, with their increased age and experience, can become more effective. One remarried woman told us, "I've discovered I can give better 'I' messages in this marriage than in my first marriage. I've lived longer, been through a lot, and know myself better. I know more about 'I' to communicate."

It is important that the listener (at this stage of the conflict) understand the issue and the importance the partner attaches to the issue. Misunderstanding can lead to escalation of the conflict, and then you have not one issue but two: (a) the original gripe; and (b) the partner's insensitivity, which in turn might escalate to a third item of conflict, (c) angry name calling that leaves hurt feelings on both sides.

If by listening, talking, asking questions, and exploring feelings, both partners can understand what each wants, needs, and feels, and how important this is, then this communication has been effective. Once this level of understanding has been reached, the couple may want to call a truce for a while, or they may be ready to go on to the next stage. Couples should learn how long to spend on this step. Some couples never move beyond it. Some couples move away from it too fast, before they fully understand the nature of each other's needs.

Eighth, you then need to ask and explore these questions: What would it take to resolve this conflict for us? What would satisfy one partner? the other partner? both of us?

Brainstorm all possible solutions, even if they seem silly. The rules of brainstorming are that nothing is rejected on the first go-round. Then discuss each of your goals and hopes in this situation. It is possible, even probable, that you will have different goals and hopes. That's OK. Then examine the brainstorm suggestions to see which would help you do what is most important to you.

The important emphasis here is on the future. Once one partner of the couple has confronted the other and after they have talked about what they are experiencing in the present because of the accumulation of past behaviors, then the question is "Where do we want to go with this matter in the future?"

Ninth, agree on what solution or combinations of solutions you will try. Come to agreement also about the length of time you will try the solution or solutions. Set a time—reasonably precise—when you will evaluate how you are doing on the attempted solution.

Tenth, kiss and make up! Celebrate! Part of the practical wisdom of marriage for a long time has been that arguing is good because it's so much fun to make up!

There is much to celebrate at the successful conclusion of a conflict. The marriage bond has survived the conflict. Perhaps the marriage bond has even been strengthened through the conflict. And, possibly, skills and confidence for dealing with future conflicts even more ably have been developed.

There is one other thing we should say about successful conflict management in marriage. Don't hesitate to seek competent outside counsel. (We recommend professional counsel. Almost never is it a good idea to ask friends to help you with a conflict.) Some persons feel it is a sign of failure to go to a counselor. Nonsense! We go to doctors and dentists when we need their help, don't we? Some people feel that they should wait until the problems are serious before seeking counseling help. Again, nonsense! Going to a good marriage counselor may help a couple to take preventative steps in their marriage, which is much easier to do than healing old hurts. Some couples feel bad if they seem to need counseling help for every conflict. But this is the way it may be for a time. One couple with whom we visited agreed that they would make two attempts to solve any conflict that troubled them. If they were unsuccessful on the second attempt, they would immediately contact their marriage counselor, hoping to get an appointment within the next forty-eight hours. Such a style was working for them at this stage of their relationship.

If conflicts are filled with hurts that fester or if the conflict seems to be going round and round and getting nowhere, then it is probably time to seek counseling aid.

By all means, do seek constructive conflict with a goal toward reconciliation and healing. As Bach and Deutsch point out, "Like DDT, irritations are not eliminated; they accumulate."[13] Resolving irritations is a relationship-building activity. Many of you reading this book are probably in the early stages of remarriage. You have before you a great opportunity. You can initiate a constructive style of conflict so that irritations do not accumulate. Conflicts can accumulate, become poison, and kill the relationship you treasure highly, or conflicts can be resolved and become the lubricant to an effective and smooth-running marriage.

Questions for Reflection

1. In what ways do you handle conflict in your present marriage?
2. How did your parents deal with conflict? What about your previous spouse? Can you recognize the different styles of dealing with conflict and the affect it has had on you and your present marriage? What feelings about conflict did you bring to this marriage?
3. What are your ground rules for conflict?

10

The Stages of Remarriage and of Stepfamilies

A s we approach the end of our conversation, we want to share something about the progression of a remarried couple and family through time. Are there "normal" stages in building a remarried family? Is this couple proceeding "normally?" Is there anything a couple can do to strengthen their couple life and their family life? Or do they just need to tough it out for a while?

As we interviewed remarried couples, we were struck with the sense of heaviness, frustration, and confusion that we noted quite frequently in couples in the early years of remarriage. This was contrasted with a sense of strength and tolerance that we often noted in some remarried couples who had been together longer. It seemed to us that this contrast was more marked than in first marriages. Coauthor Carole noted this change in her own second marriage, and so we thought it would be helpful to explore stages of remarriage for our readers.

To our surprise, we found very little information about the stages of remarriage. But we will share what we have discovered in the hope that this will be helpful to you.

The Developing Family Life in Original and Reconstituted Families

A number of students of family life have described the original family's development in a series of stages. Let's look at the stages in the original family and then the reconstituted family, as described by Esther Wald. Wald has suggested a four-stage developmental pattern for original nuclear families.

Stage I: A nuclear family is established through marriage. The primary developmental task at this stage is for the (usually) young adults who are marrying to shift their primary commitment from their family of origin to their new family unit and develop their roles in this new family.

Stage II: A two-parent, two-generation family is established as children are born or adopted and raised by parents. In this stage, the family has two complementary but opposite tasks: (a) the inclusion of each new child that comes into the family; (b) the mutual separation and individuation of parents and children as the children mature, so that they are ready for the next stage. Wald calls the failure of this second task "enmeshment"; that is, unwillingness of parent or child to separate from each other.

Stage III: The family contracts as young adult children leave home and establish independent living patterns. In this stage, the family has the task of working out the balance between attachment and detachment. Parents and young adult children need to work out freedom and responsibility issues with each other. They need also to discover caring roles for each other as separate and independent persons.

Stage IV: The couple reestablishes itself as a marital unit without children at home. In this stage, the task of the now-alone couple is to face the issue of renewal versus boredom. After the demands of parenting for years, their issue is to find points of person-to-person sharing, companionship, and personal-couple renewal.[1]

The intact family has years to develop readiness for each successive stage of family life. This provides the point at which we may contrast the reconstituted family.

Esther Wald's comment about the early tasks of remarried families is "so much, so fast."[2] She suggests that the remarried family goes through not four but seven stages, and that these stages begin at the same point as does the nuclear family—with the formation of the original marriage. Here, then, are the seven stages she suggests with regard to the remarried family:

Stage I: Establishment of the original family as described previously.

Stage II: Expansion of the original nuclear family as children are born or adopted and raised by the parents.

Stage III: Dissolution of the first marriage and family structure, either by death or divorce. The task here is to develop physical and emotional separation from one's former spouse.

Stage IV: Reorganization of the family as a single-parent unit. The developmental task here is coping versus disorganization. The task also includes mastering the responsibilities of family life with one less adult sharing in the tasks. Often in single-parent families extremely close ties develop between the remaining parent and children.

Stage V: Expansion and reorganization as a remarried-family. Two people marry (at least one of whom was formerly married) with the hope that they will continue together to old age and that new members of the family will form meaningful bonds with each other. However, these hopes encounter some extremely complex developmental tasks. We will speak more of the specific issues the remarried family may thus face, but for now we note the importance, complexity, and vastness of the tasks. This is apt to be both an important and a difficult stage of family life.

Stage VI: Launching-contraction. The tasks are the same as in Stage 3 of the original nuclear family but may be complicated by remarried family issues.

Stage VII: The marital unit without children at home. Again the tasks are similar to the fourth and final stage in the original family.[3]

All this may be interesting but what can a family expect in each of the stages after the remarried family has begun its life together (Wald's stage V)? She has obviously painted with a very broad brush because it is hard to answer that question with any precision! There is much variety in remarried families.

The way it appears to us is this. Becoming a united remarried family is like running a race. The individuals start out thinking it is a fairly level cross-country race. They soon discover, instead, that it is an obstacle course! Some of the obstacles are fairly easy to get past. The family is well prepared and negotiates those problems pretty well. Others are more formidable. Some obstacles look easy but are far from easy when the family gets to them. The analogy breaks down at this point, for on an obstacle course the runner comes upon the obstacles one by one. In remarriage, families may be dealing with several obstacles at once! Some families get hung up on these obstacles and either limp along, severely bruised, or give up and turn back. But some families make it past the obstacles and move on to some sort of unity and strength.

What are the obstacles of which we speak? Wald gives a list of suggestions, but others could be added. Some of the obstacles are:

A. *Manner of induction* into the remarried-family system. Those adults who prepare their children for the remarriage and deal with their resistance have less difficulty than those who, for some reason, do not prepare their children.

B. *Ghosts.* Ghosts (idealized memories of one's former partner and family life) may produce detrimental comparisons and make it hard for two families to meet head on and work out their relationship.

C. *Enmeshment.* Prior parent-child bonds that neither child nor parent want to relinguish may inhibit the couple's formation of a successful marriage partnership. Some new spouses confess that they feel like the "other woman," or the "other man" when around their spouse and children.

D. *Biological preference.* Because children usually have a clear preference for their biological parent over their stepparent, family development is a struggle. Stepparents may be rejected and left out of useful nurturing, disciplining, socializing tasks. This of course, can be a problem between stepparent and stepchild or between husband and wife, if one feels that the spouse is "distant" to his or her stepchildren. The family needs to understand and acknowledge that the "step" relationship, though different, is a relationship in its own right and not a poor substitute for a biological parent. Stepparents and children may need to be helped to choose freely and work out their own boundaries and the distance-closeness they want in the remarried family.

E. *Bond Shifts.* When a person adds the task of stepparenting to that of biological parenting, additional strain results. The person who is both parent and stepparent is a person of hybrid status. When a "hybrid parent," in trying to win the love of stepchildren, ignores the needs of his or her own children, the stress and strain of bond shifts are apt to occur.

F. *Split Loyalties.* These become an obstacle when a person tries to balance ties between a new marital partner and children of a prior marriage and feels pulled in both directions.

G. *Adolescent Issues.* Family therapists note that the highest number of applications for help from remarried families come in the first year of marriage. The second highest number of applications for help come from families with adolescent children. The adolescent period is turbulent in intact families as well as in remarried families. However, in remarried families it becomes a time to challenge stepparental authority in addition to parental authority. It may also be a time when the adolescent reexperiences earlier losses. The adolescent may need to deal with the grief and mourning that they thought they had resolved as young children.

H. *Launching of Young Adults.* Special turbulence may occur when young adults in remarried families prepare to leave the family. For example, when one man's eighteen-year-old daughter wanted to move out and get her own apartment, he blamed his second wife for not being motherly enough or caring enough. Therapy revealed that the man had had the unrealistic expectation that after remarriage his family would be just as it had been; he was not ready for his young adult daughter to leave. Neither daughter nor stepmother perceived the move as anything but an appropriate step toward the independence of a young adult.[4]

How long will it take for a family to get far enough through this obstacle course that they have reasonable hope of succeeding? There will be considerable variety. For most families the process will take years. (Some jars and jolts will occur from time to time even then.) We'll try to be more precise after we look at another part of this process—the stages of the relationship of the couple with each other.

Stages of a Remarried Couple in Their Relationship with Each Other

What are the stages a remarried couple experience in their relationship with each other? We will look at this topic for couples in general and then examine the special circumstances for remarried couples.

How does a couple's relationship develop? Susan Campbell offers a road map of the journey couples take toward intimacy. She suggests, that there are five stages in the couple's journey.

The first stage is "Romance." During this stage a couple is inspired by visions, illusions, and fantasies. They project a partnership with a harmonious future filled with a continuous and joyous feeling of "we-ness." The task of this period in a couple's relationship is to discover their shared possibilities and vision. The pitfalls of this stage are believing that "wishing makes it so" and denying conflict, because of the fear that conflict will destroy the couple vision.[5]

This stage ends when the couple realize that their vision is not going to be achieved easily. Perhaps it ends as they sense the need to move on to the next stage.

The second stage is the "Power Struggle." This stage begins with the recognition that the partners, as individuals or as a couple, are not who they had imagined they were. "The illusion of unity is replaced by the disillusion of disunity."[6] Division replaces vision. The couple experience differentness, difficulty, disillusionment, disappointment, anger. When the couple let up on the power struggle, they are ready for the third stage.

Stage three, which Campbell calls "Stability," begins with forgiveness. In this stage the partners come to accept each other as individual persons, each with his or her own dreams, strengths, foibles, and weaknesses. They discover that they can learn and progress from their conflicts as they begin to evolve a stable set of rules and expectations in regard to conflict and roles. The danger of this stage is the illusion of peace, the feeling that differences no longer need to be faced and negotiated.[7]

The fourth stage is "Commitment." At this point the couple accept and learn to live with both the joys and the human shortcomings of their relationship with each other. They give up trying to reform the partner and no longer feel a need to be agreeable at all costs. They are able to live with each other's differences and yet feel free to challenge each other without getting locked into another power struggle. In this stage the couple come to experience themselves as "an interdependent, synergistic 'we-system'. . . . [able] to live with life's insoluble dilemmas and paradoxes."[8] The pitfall in this stage is that the couple concentrate so hard on their own inner harmony that they do not sense the need to concern themselves with the world beyond.

Campbell's fifth stage is "Co-Creation." Here, a couple take all that they have learned in building their own partnership and attempt to apply to the world the fruit of their mutual creativity. The tasks of a couple in this stage are to become creators of their own universe, to sense their interdependence with all of life, and to work toward a more human and sane world. In such endeavors the couple need to concern themselves with balance, for a danger is that they may focus too much attention on the world and too little attention on the care and feeding of their own partnership.[9]

This, then, is Campbell's concept of the couple's journey. She readily admits that the road map is imperfect. No couple goes through each stage in order, smoothly, and with no hitches. Couples do not necessarily begin at stage one. Some couples stay at one of the stages for quite a long time because they have issues to face in mastering that stage. This is probably most true of stage two, the "Power Struggle." Some couples move in depth through each stage, while others flit from one to another and back again, perhaps dealing with several issues simultaneously. Many couples do not make it all the way through. Some stop at stages one, two, or three. Some reach stage four, "Commitment," and some even go on to stage five, "Co-Creation." It is exciting to know that such possibilities exist and that some couples actually reach those places.

Having surveyed that road map of growth to intimacy and co-creation, a couple might ask, "How do we get there? Do we simply wait? Will time bring the necessary maturity so that we become what we want to be? Or is there something we are supposed to do, some techniques we should follow?"

David and Vera Mace answer by pointing out that success in marriage requires "*effort plus insight.*"[10] Marriage must be seen as a task at which both husband and wife must work. They add, "*Marriage today can be very rewarding, but it is also very difficult; and the rewards come only to those who recognize that success in it calls for as much intelligence and skill as success in a career or in any other major enterprise.*"[11]

So far our discussion has been about *all* couples building a life of committed intimacy. How does this information relate specifically to the remarried couple? One remarried woman told us, "I think remarried couples go through the same stages as other couples, but with a bit of cynicism." She might also have said "hesitancy" or "fearfulness," referring to the fear of failure and the need for self-protection.

Another person described the stages in his remarried relationship in terms similar to those we have just described: "First stage—euphoria; second stage—settling in; third stage—doubts; fourth stage—tentative comfort. My experience from my previous marriage both heightens the experience and makes it more difficult."

Another remarried person felt that the increased age of the marriage partners would contribute to the maturity of a second-marriage relationship. She wrote, "Instead of handling problems of marriage like a twenty-year-old, I'm handling them like a thirty-seven-year-old. I view things differently. Not the same things hurt or bug me. I hope this maturity can lead this marriage to a deeper intimacy."

Many persons commented on the fact that remarriages were difficult to maintain in the early years. It appears to us that many couples get to Campbell's stage two, the "Power Struggle," but because they have not learned to handle conflict openly and satisfyingly, they stay in an "underground" power struggle for years. One wife commented to us, "I'm so darn discouraged. Marriage is hell to begin with, and remarriage is ten times worse!" In recent contacts with this person, we note that she has moved beyond this mood and feels more hopeful about her remarried relationship.

A couple face crises together as they build their couple relationship. Perhaps one individual faces crises in which the spouse is either helpful and supportive or not. We do not want to sound overly pessimistic, but the needs of aging parents and adolescent or young-adult children, health issues, career changes, and geographical moves all do come up from time to time. And so a couple's strength may be touched and challenged more frequently in a second marriage than in a first.

Coauthor Carole is in the fourth year of her remarriage. Here are some of her reflections as she looks back over those four years. "It gets easier the longer you hang in there. I'm disgusted right now, but even this low spot doesn't feel like the end of the marriage, but it would have a few years ago. I have moved from feeling I'm going to fail to thinking I won't. I know I can make it by myself if I have to, and so this feels like a marriage of choice not necessity.

"Less than two years after we were married, my husband, Henry, was transferred approximately two hundred miles from our former home. This created all sorts of upset with the kids, leaving their biological father. It was decision time for me; did I want to stay with it? Our marriage was strengthened because of our—the kids' and mine—commitment to go.

"When we were married, I kept my maiden name. (I had gone back to it after my divorce.) But now, four years later, I don't mind if people call me by Henry's name. I am more likely to use Henry's name than I used to be. Maybe that's a true acceptance of being married."

As we explored her feelings, it occurred to us that perhaps the boundary between not being married and being married is much more vague for remarried people. In first marriages, there is often a clear initiation that announces the change of status from single to married. In first marriages this step is taken with the confidence that the marriage bond will endure. Although the second marriage has a wedding and a definite time when families come together, remarried persons may not "feel married." Oh, they know that a ceremony took place, but they also know that a number of problems have come up since they felt the attraction that first drew them together. The time comes, later on, when they begin to "feel married, for better or for worse." That's the way it was with Carole. After the family had survived a number of crises and problems, had invested a lot of effort and sharing, and had grown together, she felt a quiet confidence that, "This marriage is going to make it."

We were puzzled by the fact that when couples discussed "making it" in remarriage, they frequently mentioned the time frame of four or five years. For example, forty percent of all remarriages end in the first four years. The counsel often given by an experienced person, one who has been remarried for a long time, to a newly remarried person is, "Give it a chance, it will be better in five years or so." Given the vastness of the tasks in remarriage, that may be the minimum time needed for the couple to make that final commitment.

In remarriage, two people find each other and then decide to marry. Either or both bring their families with them. Simultaneously, they build a couple relationship and a family relationship (though each family member resists or cooperates and proceeds at his or her own speed). All of this is terribly complicated, and thus the building of the new family may be incredibly difficult. For those floundering in the task, the word comes from more experienced remarried pioneers, "Don't give up. The one-flesh marriage is possible. Sure, it will take more time, attention, and effort than it seemed at first, but the rewards are great. Hang in there."

Questions for Reflection

1. Which of the obstacles cited by Wald have been the most difficult for your remarried family?
2. At what stage in a couple's journey are you?
3. When did you feel truly "married"?

11

Long-Term Issues in Remarriage

So far we have spoken primarily of issues that need to be faced early in the remarriage. Now we turn to issues remarried couples may face as they live out their lives together.

Issues the Remarried Couple May Face Sometime in Their Relationship

Illness of a Child

Shortly after coauthor Carole was remarried (her former husband had remarried earlier than she), her daughter Kelly became ill with a blood disease. For days Kelly was in the hospital, the diagnosis, treatment, and prognosis of her disease uncertain. Since her parents and stepparents all lived in the same community, quite often four concerned adults were all in the hospital room with Kelly. Carole recalls the confusion of doctors and nurses over this. Who were Kelly's mother and father? Who was married to whom? To whom were they to give information? Who should be asked to sign permission forms?

Carole remembers a particularly low moment when the outcome was still unclear. She was walking down the hall with her former husband and crying, "I wish it were me." He reached out and touched her shoulder in tentative emotional support. She appreciated this act of caring but was still uncertain whether all four adults were in this together. In such a time, who could be counted on for emotional support? Who could not be asked for such support? Information, decisions, support to the child, support to the adults—all had to be worked out by a group of four adults rather than by a couple.

The practical matter of finances is also an issue when a child is ill. Since the biological father often still carries the children on his insurance, the biological mother and biological father need to work together in the cumbersome matters of dealing with insurance companies. Then they need to decide how the uncovered expense is to be paid.

Kelly has recovered and is now a happy, healthy young woman. But Carole still recalls the difficult time when the two remarried couples had to work together more closely than they were prepared to do.

Death of a Child

After Henry and Carole had been married for three years, they received the tragic news that Henry's twenty-three-year-old son Mike had been killed. They decided that services for Mike should be held in Henry's former home community, where he had met and married his first wife. It also seemed appropriate for Mike to be buried in the cemetery plot with his mother, Henry's first wife.

Making most of the decisions seemed to fall on Henry's shoulders while he was also absorbing the cruel blow of his son's murder. He knew that his wife, Carole, and his stepchildren cared for him and supported him. But he and his son and daughter-in-law, Hank and Judy, seemed to bear the heaviest load. It meant he had to return to the grave of his first wife, Phyllis, and reopen the grief wounds from her death at the same time he was experiencing his fresh grief for Mike. This was tempered slightly by returning to his little central Wisconsin home town and being upheld by lifetime friends in familiar surroundings. It was tempered also by the presence and support of his older son, Hank, and daughter-in-law, Judy.

For Carole, many things swirled around at once. Foremost was her compassion for her husband, whose depth of grief she could not share completely, since Mike's birth, childhood, youth, and young-adult years had not been hers to share with Henry. She also felt grief over the loss of her budding friendship with Mike. She realized the need to help her three children deal with their grief over the loss of their stepbrother. And she was apprehensive about going back to Henry's original home as his wife, since that was the community that had known and loved, and now vividly remembered, Henry's first wife. It was a difficult time for all of them.

In the months after Mike's death, Carole struggled with knowing how to be comforting, supportive, or even in touch with what her husband was going through. She was uncertain, also, as to how much help to give with the necessary correspondence and legal matters. Although she loved her husband, Mike had been *his* son, and so the responsibility and decisions were his.

For Carole's friend, who lost a young-adult son in an accidental death, the issue was quite different. The friend was divorced, but neither she nor her former husband had yet remarried. Carole remembers the difficulty she observed as two estranged people, who had both dearly loved their son, had to work through the decisions about casket, service, burial, finances, and other issues with each other. Two persons who had decided that they could not deal with each other in day-to-day decisions were forced to work together to make some of the most painful decisions they would ever have to make.

A Child in Difficulty

Still another time when remarried people may need to deal with former spouses is when a child is in difficulty.

Glenn, a remarried husband with whom we spoke, recalled, ''When Jenny, my first wife, and I broke up, we had very few dealings with each other. Our older children seemed to accept the break-up and my remarriage to Lucy pretty well. But not Dawn, who was thirteen at the time. She wasn't happy anywhere. She would stay in my home for a while, get mad and go live with her mother for a while, and then be back. Finally, Dawn decided she didn't want anything to do with either of us, and so she ran off to live with her boyfriend. She was seventeen at the time. This was very much against both her mother's and my values. I felt it was time to talk with my former wife. After she and I talked things out, we were able to give Dawn a clear, united message: we disapproved of her actions, but we still loved her. If she wanted to find other alternatives for living, we'd help her. Dawn still hasn't responded. But at least Jenny and I aren't blaming each other. At least we don't feel that we are contributing further to Dawn's confusion.''

Glenn's story expresses some of the courses of action that remarried people may choose if an adolescent or young-adult child gets into difficulty. Do you

—let the child live with the consequences of his or her action?

—bail him or her out?

—give the child one more chance but let him or her know after this he or she is on his or her own?

These are not easy questions, but if two parents give different answers, undercut one another, and blame one another, the child in trouble will probably flounder all the more. For the welfare of the child and for the serenity of the adults involved, persons must learn how to deal openly and honestly in such strife-filled situations.

Now we can go on to happier matters.

Birthdays, Holidays, Graduations, and Times of Achievement

Wise are the parents/stepparents who have learned to work together so that such events are happy experiences for all concerned, not occasions for battles. Holidays (Christmas, for example) need to be coordinated so that children can have special times with each part of their family and adults can have their times of celebration as well. Gifts may need to be discussed and coordinated. Parents/stepparents should not use gifts as ammunition in their battle to outdo other adults in the children's lives.

There will be times (graduations, recitals, concerts, plays, athletic events, etc.) when the child may want to have all the significant adults in his or her life share in his or her achievement. Wise adults know that the child's happiness in the achievement is increased if significant adults are there to support, applaud, congratulate, or celebrate with the child.

Wise adults will not set up competitions that disturb the child's happiness. They will not force the child to choose between going with one set of parents or the other.

Changing Financial Circumstances

As children become youths and then young adults, their hobbies, education, recreation, clothing, and so on, escalate in cost. Further, steady increases in the cost of living mean that the basic costs of raising children are greater every year.

However, the amount of child support provided by the absent spouse does not increase automatically. Such support will stay the same unless the couple decide, negotiate, or agree—either voluntarily or as the result of a court-ordered adversary settlement—to increase the support. One wife told us, ''My ex-husband and I get along pretty well, except when we have to discuss money matters for the kids. I know he cares about the children, but he feels pressure to provide well for his new wife and stepchildren also.'' Biological parents need to keep the lines of communication open so they can discuss a financial plan beneficial to all involved.

Weddings of Children and Stepchildren

Very probably, some day your children or stepchildren will want to get married. If they want a public wedding ceremony, the marrying couple and their families face lots of decisions. Weddings have many traditions, and almost all of these traditions are built upon the assumption that families are intact.

Sometimes weddings become battlegrounds between the bride's or groom's estranged parents. For example, a recent Ann Landers column contained a letter in which a divorced mother of the bride raised some questions. Divorced five years previously, the mother had had the daughter with her most of the time. When the daughter discussed wedding plans with her father and his new wife, her father said that wedding invitations would have to be issued in his name and the name of his new wife. The bride's mother's name would not appear. The bride had to dress at her father's home and he and his new wife would have the seats at the wedding appropriate to the father and mother of the bride. When the daughter objected that this was unfair to her mother, the father responded, ''If your mother wants to be part of it, she will have to pay for half.'' The bride's mother went on to say that she couldn't afford it, that she was already buying the wedding gown and making some of the bridesmaids' dresses. She asked Ann for advice.

Landers responded,

> The invitations should read: ''Marian Doe and John Doe request your presence at the marriage of their daughter Jane to _____.''
> You and your ex should be seated together in the church, and the new wife should be gracious enough to sit with friends. And Jane should dress wherever she chooses.[1]

We think Ann Landers responded too rigidly. We will mention some other options shortly.

Esther Wald tells of a family who came to her for therapy. The event that caused them to seek help was a wedding. Though Mr. and Mrs. Maynor had been married for seven years, the seating arranged by Mr. Maynor's son Mike (the groom) clearly assigned the present Mrs. Maynor second-class status. It seemed to express Mike's hope that his divorced and remarried parents would still get back together.[2] We can imagine that the tensions floating around that wedding caused it to be much less happy than weddings are supposed to be.

How can weddings that have a maximum of celebration and a minimum of unhealthy tension be planned in remarried families? This is possible when the marrying couple, their parents, and their stepparents hold healthy, open discussions about their feelings and needs.

We think that they can make a variety of decisions that will be appropriate. These decisions will not be the same in every family because many factors are involved. For example, how long has the stepparent been married to the bride's or groom's parent? How deep is the relationship between stepparent and stepchild? How important to the stepparent are the matters of seating and participation with the spouse in the wedding? A number of issues should be discussed until there is agreement, or at least acceptance and clarity. Here are examples of other issues the couple and families must resolve.

—Whose names go on wedding announcements and invitations? Should only the names of the biological parents be used, or have the stepparents been so much a part of the bride's or groom's life that their names should be included?

—Who pays? Some discussion needs to be carried on about what the expenses will be. Weddings that are beautiful and enjoyable can range from inexpensive to costly. The best celebration for anyone is the one that fits the couple and does not leave them, or anyone else, in serious debt after it is over. What would the couple like to have for their wedding and celebration? Is the request reasonable and affordable? What are their parents and stepparents able and willing to do? (How many of these adults are generating incomes? What about the couple itself?) Perhaps one couple will offer to take care of flowers, music, and expenses at the church; another will pay for the wedding clothing; another, the rehearsal dinner; another, the wedding reception. The possibilities are endless (as are the details that need to be worked out)!

—Who walks the bride down the aisle if she desires parental escort? Father (even if he hasn't seen her much lately)? Stepfather? We know at least one wedding at which the bride—at her wish—went down the aisle between her father and stepfather. Both men were magnanimous enough to share this moment with the other.

—Where do parents and stepparents sit during the wedding? Do the mother and father of the bride (or groom) still sit together in the front row even though no longer married to each other? Should that row include their new spouses? Or should stepparents be given hosting tasks such as being in charge of the guest book, ushering, welcoming?

—Who stands in the receiving line?

—If there is assigned seating at a wedding dinner, where are bride's and/or groom's stepparents seated?

We have known couples who worried about the tensions that might be caused by the fact that their parents had not been together for some time. It is important to help the couple to put such worries aside by telling them, "Your happiness is so important to us that we want your wedding day to be perfect. Don't worry about us. We'll be just fine."

Birth and Dedication/Christening/Baptism of Grandchildren

As at other special occasions, the remarried person will want to have a solid, trusting relationship with the present spouse and an accepting, noncombative attitude toward the former spouse. Then all can enter cooperatively into the celebration of a new life and the joy of new parents.

Needs of Aging Parents

One wife told us, "In my first marriage, I complained a lot about my husband's parents. It seemed to me that they interfered a lot and that he let them. He seemed never to have become independent of them. In my second marriage, it's different. I don't complain, and my husband isn't dependent on his widowed mother. But she's dependent on him. She needs a good bit of his attention and money, and she'll probably need more in the years ahead. But I seem to be able to accept this better and don't begrudge what he gives her."

Nothing stays the same. Many persons in midlife will find that while the needs of their maturing children decrease, the needs of aging parents will probably increase. Ongoing communication will be needed to help the couple be in touch with each other about their parents' changing needs so that they can accept and support each other in responding to these needs.

Death and Burial of Family Members

The death of Henry's son caused Henry and Carole to be aware of another long-term issue they had to face. Where would each of them be buried? This issue is more likely to arise when at least one partner is widowed.

Henry chose to have his son buried in the same family plot as Henry's first wife, Mike's mother. Henry had secured a family burial plot, had bought a family gravestone, and had buried his first wife and his son there. He expected that one day his body would be placed there too. A question then occurred to them: "Where would Carole want to be buried? Probably not in the same plot, but where?"

The tragedy had forced on Henry and Carole a question that many avoid. To save the added heartbreak of conflicts and disagreements among survivors after one's death, one's wishes and plans in this matter should be discussed and made known. Does each desire burial or cremation? Where? These decisions need to be clear.

One remarried women (both she and her present husband were widowed and had family burial plots) told us how she and her husband worked out plans in regard to burial. "We decided that we preferred to be cremated. As years have passed we have become more comfortable and trusting with each other. We have told all our kids about our decision. I can now accept that if my husband dies first, it might give comfort to his kids to have his ashes buried in their family plot. (The 'comfort of the living' has been our guideline.) At least I will want to talk with his children (who are now my friends) about any feelings they may have. It's not a problem any more. The disposal of my body doesn't feel religiously important to me. I would want my husband to do whatever gives *him* comfort first of all. If he and the children can both feel good about it, even better."

Throughout the couple's life together, the couple face challenges that are also opportunities to support each other and to strengthen their life together.

Questions for Reflection

1. Have the parents and stepparents in your family system planned together so that special holidays and family occasions will not cause conflicts?

2. What financial problems do you foresee in the future? How will you deal with these?

3. What do you see as the strengths in your remarriage? What are the issues that you need to work on?

Build on the strengths!

Work on the weaknesses!

12

And Finally

Earlier in the book we suggested to you that a path to strength in remarriage includes the following:
—Face the issues in remarriage;
—Make the problems and disagreements visible;
—Make visible the strengths you feel as a couple;
—Discuss and negotiate differences.
We hope that the preceding chapters have helped you begin to use this process on a wide range of issues.

During the time that we have been working on this book, coauthor Carole has experienced a great deal in her remarriage. There have been predictable problems, unexpected crises (an unanticipated move), many arguments, a tragedy (the death of Henry's son), ups and downs, blue moments and celebrations, and a slowly maturing strength in their relationship. As a result of her own experience and conversations with other remarried persons, some of her convictions have been strengthened and others have emerged.

We believe that remarriage and blended families are viable life-styles. In 1980, one in every seven families in America was a blended family. As an American family type, the stepfamily is coming of age. It deserves attention and care, the same as any other kind of family.

We believe that no family is perfect and that all families, original families or stepfamilies, have their problems. Therefore, it is a mistake to consider a stepfamily a second-rate family. Some people tend to blame everything they do not like about the family on the fact that it is a stepfamily.

We believe that God forgives failure in personal life and in relationships. We believe that God forgives and accepts persons who have undergone divorce and remarriage. We believe that both divorce and remarriage may be appropriate decisions. We believe that God is a God of resurrection and rebirth. This God of new beginnings will bless and grant to couples who seek it, a new beginning.

We believe that a new marriage and a new family are, therefore, very special gifts. Carole recalls that in her first marriage she assumed she'd be married to her husband for the rest of her life; so she ignored, denied, and postponed problems that should have been dealt with, until they overwhelmed her. Being remarried offers a person a chance to develop a new relationship, the one he or she has always longed for. Remarriage provides another chance to work at building and nurturing a good relationship.

We believe that the remarried couple and stepfamily must undertake many developmental tasks early in the marriage. Confusion and discouragement are to be expected as persons attempt to build relationships with each other, each other's children, and each other's families, all at once. New roles, rules, tasks, living arrangements, and systems, all have to be negotiated. We believe that the colloquial advice ''Give it time . . . . Hang in there'' is inspired and that no one should withdraw precipitously during the early years of a remarriage. The struggles of individuals, couple, and family are, quite likely, very normal. Many families experience a difficult adjustment in the early stages of remarriage.

We believe that blended families have to work hard at building a satisfying married life. We believe that the effort and attention are worthwhile investments.

We believe that every blended family is unique. Two families with past histories merge in a new way. The individuals involved come together at varying rates as family life develops in bumps and starts. These individuals are also going through their own aging, processes, life stages, and developmental tasks. These tasks may enhance or conflict with family life.

We believe that every remarried couple will have unexpected problems and unexpected joys. Though both partners may try very hard to understand the other completely and to work through all issues before their marriage, they will have some surprises. But that's OK. We believe that the developing relationship can be strong enough to absorb such surprises.

We believe that although relationships develop slowly and cannot be forced, they do develop. Stepparent-stepchild and stepsibling relationships can develop until they are cherished and valued by all. This is particularly true if the adults are mature enough to give the children freedom to love all the parental figures in their lives and if individuals do not push ''love expectations'' onto unready persons.

We believe that remarried persons can benefit from the support of others. Other remarried couples, counselors, and the church can all be rich resources, so that couples do not have to develop their life-styles in isolation.

We believe that couples and families should feel free to ask for help. Early aid can be educational and preventative and can help ward off deep, long-term issues later on.

We believe that one of the skills most needed in marriage, and especially in remarriage, is how to manage conflict so that no one is put down and everyone wins. A new marriage is a good time *not* to build a pile of resentments. Conflicts kept current and resolved with love can become deep, bonding experiences in marriage.

We believe that every remarried couple should keep as its highest priority and most basic task the nourishing of their couple relationship. They should identify what they need to keep that mutual bond alive and growing, and they should make provision for whatever they need to do this. Ultimately this process will serve other members of the family as well, for a strong couple relationship will be a source of strength in the conflicts, problems, and crises that inevitably come to every family.

We believe that remarried couples are included in that biblical ideal ''Therefore a man leaves his father and his mother and cleaves to his wife and they become one flesh'' (Genesis 2:24, RSV). We believe that the Bible vision of ''one flesh'' refers to a process of dynamic becoming as two individuals work at sharing joys, sorrows, dreams, goals, and daily routines. Perhaps, in time, other family members will join in a joyous sense of unity with the husband and wife of the household. A young man in one of the families with whom Esther Wald worked put it well. Said

Tom, "[We are] no longer a house of strangers, but instead [we are] beginning to be a house of friends."[1]

We dare to hope that such progress can be true for many remarried families and that you and your family will be among them. Encouraging couples and families to go on and seek that richer life together is exciting.

Through inspiration, perspiration, concentration, perpetuation, and by the power and grace of God, may your marriage become "one flesh" and your family a "house of friends!"

Notes

Chapter 1

[1]Emily B. Visher and John S. Visher, *Stepfamilies: A Guide to Working with Stepparents and Stepchildren* (Secaucus, N.J.: Citadel Press, 1979), pp. xviii, 5, 48.

[2]*Ibid.*, p. 5.

[3]Anne W. Simon, *Stepchild in the Family* (New York: The Bobbs-Merrill Co., Inc., Odyssey Press, 1964) p. 17, quoted in Visher and Visher, *Stepfamilies*, p. 5.

[4]Visher and Visher, *Stepfamilies*, p. 32.

Chapter 2

[1]James J. Young, personal correspondence.

[2]Quoted in James J. Young, *Growing Through Divorce* (Ramsey, N.J.: Paulist Press, 1979), p. 31.

[3]John T. Catoir, *Catholics and Broken Marriage* (Notre Dame: Ave Maria Press, 1979), p. 51.

[4]*Ibid.*, p. 53.

[5]*Ibid.*, p. 55.

[6]G. Edwin Bontrager, *Divorce and the Faithful Church* (Scottsdale, Pa.: Herald Press, 1978), p. 81.

Chapter 4

[1]Mel Krantzler, *Learning to Love Again* (New York: Harper & Row, Publishers, Inc., Thomas Y. Crowell, 1977), p. 3.

[2]Bruce Fisher, *Rebuilding: When Your Relationship Ends* (San Luis Obispo, Calif.: Impact Publishers, 1981), pp. 99-104.

[3]Myron Chartier, personal letter.

[4]Fisher, *Rebuilding*, p. 17.

[5]James D. Whitehead, *Marrying Well: Possibilities in Christian Marriage Today* (New York: Doubleday & Co., Inc., 1981), p. 357. Exerpt from Evelyn L. Whitehead and copyright © by Evelyn L. Whitehead. Reprinted by permission of Doubleday & Co., Inc.

[6]See James Emerson, *Divorce, the Church and Remarriage* (Philadelphia: The Westminster Press, 1961).

[7]Fisher, *Rebuilding*, p. 141.

[8]Krantzler, *Learning to Love Again*, p. 85.

[9]*Ibid.*, *p. 90.*

[10]*Ibid.*, p. 92.

[11]Many churches are now providing support groups for those whose spouses have died and for those who have been divorced. Some church social agencies, such as Lutheran Social Services, also offer such groups. Many communities have a local unit of *Parents Without Partners*.

Chapter 5

[1]Morton M. Hunt, *The World of the Formerly Married* (New York: McGraw-Hill, Inc., 1966), pp. 112-113. Used by permission.

[2]*Ibid.*, p. 136.

[3]*Ibid.*, p. 185-195.

[4]*Ibid.*, p. 142-170.

[5]Mel Krantzler, *Learning to Love Again* (New York: Harper & Row, Publishers, Inc., Thomas Y. Crowell, 1977), p. 124.

[6]*Ibid.*, p. 141.

[7]George R. Bach and Ronald M. Deutsch, *Pairing* (New York: Peter H. Wyden, Inc., 1970), p. 7.

[8]*Ibid.*, p. 12.

[9]*Ibid.*, p. 13.

[10]Laura J. Singer, *Stages: The Crises That Shape Your Marriage* (New York: Grosset & Dunlap, Inc., 1980), p. 31.

[11]*Ibid.*, p. 48.

[12]Virginia Satir, *Peoplemaking* (Palo Alto, Calif.: Science and Behavior Books, 1972), p. 133.

[13]Krantzler, *Learning to Love Again*, p. 153.

[14]Singer, *Stages*, pp. 40-41.

[15]Satir, *Peoplemaking*, p. 135. Reprinted by permission of the author and publisher. Virginia Satir, *Peoplemaking*. 1972, Science and Behavior Books, Inc., Palo Alto, CA, USA.

[16]Emily B. Visher and John S. Visher, *Stepfamilies: A Guide to Working with Stepparents and Stepchildren* (Secaucus, N.J.: Citadel Press, 1979), pp. 121-140.

[17]Clifford J. Sager, *et al.*, *Treating The Remarried Family* (New York: Brunner/Mazel, 1983), pp. 66-72.

Chapter 6

[1]Emily B. Visher and John S. Visher, *How to Win as a Stepfamily* (New York: Dembner Books, 1982), p. 2.

[2]Andrew Cherlin, "Remarriage as an Incomplete Institution," *American Journal of Sociology* (1978), vol. 84, no. 3, pp. 634-650.

[3]Lucile Duberman, *The Reconstituted Family: A Study of Remarried Couples and Their Children* (Chicago: Nelson-Hall Publishers, 1975), p. 8.

[4]Frederick Capaldi and Barbara McRae, *Stepfamilies: A Cooperative Responsibility* (New York: Franklin Watts Inc., New Viewpoints/Vision Books, 1979), p. 52.

[5]Visher and Visher, *How to Win as a Stepfamily*, pp. 7-8.

[6]*Ibid.*, p. 7.

[7]See Ivan Boszormenyi-Nagy and Geraldine Spark, *Invisible Loyalties* (New York: Harper & Row, Publishers, Inc., 1973).

[8]J. C. Wynn, *Family Therapy in Pastoral Ministry* (San Francisco: Harper & Row, Publishers, Inc., 1982), pp. 37-50.

[9]Ruth Roosevelt and Jeannette Lofas, *Living in Step* (New York: McGraw-Hill, Inc., 1977), p. 78.

[10]Quoted in Mel Krantzler, *Learning to Love Again* (New York: Harper & Row, Publishers, Inc., Thomas Y. Crowell, 1977), p. 219.

[11]Visher and Visher, *How to Win as a Stepfamily*, pp. 13-14.

[12]Virginia Satir, *Peoplemaking* (Palo Alto, Calif.: Science and Behavior Books, 1972), p. 174.

[13]*Ibid.*, pp. 174-175.

[14]*Ibid.*, p. 175.

[15]*Ibid.*, p. 123. Reprinted by permission of the author and publisher. Virginia Satir, *Peoplemaking*. 1972, Science and Behavior Books, Inc., Palo Alto, CA, USA.

Chapter 7

[1]Emily B. Visher and John S. Visher, *Stepfamilies: A Guide to Working With Stepparents and Stepchildren* (Secaucus, N.J.: Citadel Press, 1979), pp. 139-140.

[2]Virginia Satir, *Peoplemaking* (Palo Alto, Calif.: Science and Behavior Books, 1972), pp. 148-153.

[3]Ruth Roosevelt and Jeannette Lofas, *Living in Step* (New York: McGraw-Hill, Inc., 1976), p. 116.

[4]Esther Wald, *The Remarried Family: Challenge and Promise* (New York: Family Service Association of America, 1981), p. 92.

[5]Emily B. Visher and John S. Visher, *How to Win as a Stepfamily* (New York: Dembner Books, 1982), p. 80.

[6]Lucile Duberman, *The Reconstituted Family* (Chicago: Nelson-Hall Publishers, 1975), p. 107. She is citing Leonard Benson, *The Family Bond* (New York: Random House, Inc., 1971), pp. 9-13.

[7]*Ibid.*, pp. 109-110.

[8]Fredrick Capaldi and Barbara McRae, *Stepfamilies: A Cooperative Responsibility* (New York: Franklin Watts, Inc., New Viewpoints/Vision Books, 1979), p. 123.

[9]*Ibid.*, pp. 124-126.

[10]Luree Nicholson and Laura Torbet, *How to Fight Fair with Your Kids . . . and Win!* (New York: Harcourt Brace Jovanovich, Inc., 1980), p. 276.

[11]Laura J. Singer, *Stages: The Crises That Shape Your Marriage* (New York: Grosset and Dunlap, Inc., 1980), p. 132.

[12]*Ibid.*, p. 133.

[13]*Ibid.*, p. 133.

[14]*Ibid.*, p. 158.

[15]Emily B. Visher and John S. Visher, *How to Win as a Stepfamily* (New York: Dembner Books, 1982), pp. 53-54.

[16]Visher and Visher, *Stepfamilies*, p. 47.

[17]Visher and Visher, *How to Win as a Stepfamily*, p. 55.

[18]*Ibid.*, pp. 55-56.

[19]Duberman,*The Reconstituted Family*, p. 113.

[20]Visher and Visher, *How to Win as a Stepfamily*, p. 88.

[21]Roosevelt and Lofas, *Living in Step*, p. 154.

[22]Wald, *The Remarried Family*, p. 109.

[23]Roosevelt and Lofas, *Living in Step*, p. 96.

[24]Wald, *The Remarried Family*, pp. 109-110. Reprinted from *The Remarried Family*, by Esther Wald, by permission of the publisher. Copyright 1981, Family Service Association of America.

[25]Quoted in Visher and Visher, *Stepfamilies*, p. 117.

[26]Roosevelt and Lofas, *Living in Step*, p. 155.

Chapter 8

[1]Lucile Duberman, *The Reconstituted Family: A Study of Remarried Couples and Their Children* (Chicago: Nelson-Hall Publishers, 1975), p. 40.

[2]Lillian Messinger, "Remarriage Between Divorced People with Children from Previous Marriages: A Proposal for Preparation for Remarriage," *Journal of Marriage and Family Counseling*, vol. 2, no. 2 (April 1976), p. 197.

[3]Paul G. Schurman, *Money Problems and Pastoral Care* (Philadelphia: Fortress Press, 1982), p. 4.

[4]*Ibid.*, p. 6.

[5]Sylvia Porter, *Sylvia Porter's Money Book* (New York: Avon Books, 1975, 1976), p. 10. Copyright © 1975 by Sylvia Porter. Reprinted by permission of Doubleday & Co., Inc.

[6]Schurman, *Money Problems and Pastoral Care*, p. 18.

[7]Porter, *Sylvia Porter's Money Book*, p. 12.

[8]*Ibid.*, p. 13.

[9]*Ibid.*, p. 16.

[10]*Ibid.*, p. 17.

[11]*Ibid.*, p. 19.

[12]*Ibid.*, p. 32.

[13]*Ibid.*, pp. 21-22.

[14]*Ibid.*, p. 725.

[15]*Ibid.*, pp. 726-727.

[16]Ruth Roosevelt and Jeannette Lofas, *Living in Step* (New York: McGraw-Hill, Inc., 1976, 1977), pp. 92.

[17]*Ibid.*, pp. 91-92.

[18]Emily B. Visher and John S. Visher, *Stepfamilies: A Guide to Working with Stepparents and Stepchildren* (Secaucus, N.J.: Citadel Press, 1979), p. 101.

[19]Schurman, *Money Problems and Pastoral Care*, p. 22.

[20]*Ibid.*, pp. 22-23.

[21]Jessie Bernard, *Remarriage: A Study of Marriage* (New York: Russell and Russell, Publishers, 1956, 1971), p. 189.

[22]Jeff Herrigan and Jackie Herrigan, *Loving Free: How Our Marriage Works* (New York: Grosset and Dunlap, Inc., 1973), p. 211.

[23]*Ibid.*, p. 241.

[24]*Ibid.*, p. 242.

[25]*Ibid.*, p. 243.

Chapter 9

[1]David Johnson, *Reaching Out* (Englewood Cliffs, N.J.: Prentice-Hall, Inc., 1972), p. 164.

²John Scanzoni, *Love and Negotiate: Creative Conflict in Marriage* (Waco, Tex.: Word Inc., 1979), p. 62.

³David Augsburger, *Caring Enough to Confront* (Glendale, Calif.: Regal Books, G/L Publications, 1980), p. 11.

⁴Johnson, *Reaching Out*, p. 203.

⁵Quoted in Jacqueline Carr, *Communicating and Relating* (Menlo Park, Calif.: The Benjamin/Cummings Publishing Co., Inc., 1979), p. 385. Used by permission.

⁶Shirley Halleen, "Basic Skills for Conflict Management" (unpublished paper), pp. 1-2.

⁷Augsburger, *Caring Enough to Confront*, p. 40.

⁸Johnson, *Reaching Out*, p. 160.

⁹Quoted in Augsburger, *Caring Enough to Confront*, p. 20.

¹⁰*Ibid.*, p. 15.

¹¹George R. Bach and Ronald M. Deutsch, *Pairing* (New York: Peter H. Wyden, Inc., 1970), pp. 61, 59.

¹²Some of these suggestions have come from all of the above cited sources, but most specifically from Bach and Deutsch, *Pairing*, pp. 149-150 and George R. Bach and Peter H. Wyden, *The Intimate Enemy* (New York: Avon Books, 1968), pp. 56-102.

¹³Bach and Deutsch, *Pairing*, p. 133.

Chapter 10

¹Esther Wald, *The Remarried Family: Challenge and Promise* (New York: Family Service Association of America, 1981), pp. 116-117.

²*Ibid.*, p. 113.

³*Ibid.*, pp. 118-141.

⁴*Ibid.*, pp. 127-140.

⁵Susan Campbell, *The Couple's Journey* (San Luis Obispo, Calif.: Impact Publishers, 1980), pp. 10, 14-15.

⁶*Ibid.*, p. 11.

⁷*Ibid.*, pp. 12, 14-15.

⁸*Ibid.*, pp. 12-14.

⁹*Ibid.*, pp. 13-15.

¹⁰David and Vera Mace, *We Can Have Better Marriages* (Nashville: Abindgon Press, 1974), p. 73.

¹¹*Ibid.*, pp. 65, 73.

Chapter 11

¹*Racine Journal Times* (November 20, 1982), p. 9A.

²Esther Wald, *The Remarried Family: Challenge and Promise* (New York: Family Service Association of America, 1981), pp. 201-209.

Chapter 12

¹Esther Wald, *The Remarried Family: Challenge and Promise* (New York: Family Service Association of America, 1981), p. 201.

DATE